THE NEXT LEVEL

Mary Anne

Rise To The Next Level

ANNIEPRESS.COM

Published by Annie Press, a woman-owned company in Wisconsin, specializing in publishing materials with a purpose and promoting a "give-back" attitude. Charitable donations are given for every book sale.

 Most Annie Press books are available at special quantity discounts for bulk purchase for fund-raising, events, sales promotions (retail), book clubs, and educational needs. **Please use our website, ANNIEPRESS.COM, for all inquiries, feedback, and requests.**

DISCLAIMER: The author and publisher offer this book in hopes that the author's experiences and opinions assist others in all ways; it is not based on any professional or medical training of any kind. The author and publisher does not dispense medical advice or other professional advice, or prescribe the use of any technique or diet or healing modality as a form of diagnosis or treatment for anything, be it spiritual, physical, emotional, mental or the like for any being. The author is simply sharing personal knowledge that may be helpful to others. The author, publisher, and associates (including references made in this book) make no claims or guarantees and cannot be held responsible or liable for any results, actions or lack of actions, or damages or losses or consequences of any kind. In life, we are all responsible for our own choices, including what consult we use for the wellness of our mind, body, and soul.

Book Topics: Health, Mind, & Body, Life Enrichment, Awareness, Personal Growth, Relationships, Spirituality, Wisconsin Author

ISBN-13: 978-0-9817983-5-6

Dedication

To my dear first grandchild, a beaming example of joyfully living life in the present moment, savoring all people and things in current view. The vast knowledge, perspective, and clarity is naturally soul-to-soul, what we all so longingly yearn for.

I've never had anyone tell me they love me so often and mean it, so unconditionally.

I hope we laugh at life, be silly, and sing and dance and play together forever! May we all do our absolute best to support your true essence, your whole life. Love you to the moon and back a million, ba-yllion, trillion times!

TABLE OF CONTENTS – BY TOPIC

Relationships

Letting Go

Awareness

Change

Difficult Situations

Self-Love

Health

TABLE OF CONTENTS – BY ARTICLE DATE

INTRODUCTION

When I released my first book, **RISE ABOVE THE SH**! Down-to-earth thinking from Wisconsin**, I had no idea how my life would explode! That book was the result of one triggering thought: There has to be more to life than this! I was answered, with ways to overcome over 50 common things that hold us back from who we are really meant to be, and with that, how our lives are meant to be, and despite my reserved nature, I was compelled to share it with the world, in the form of a book.

I learned early on, that sharing these thoughts helps to keep me in check; it serves as a great reminder as to the way I really want to live my life. As we strive to become more of our real self, life has a way of opening up so it can show us the real beauty in everything. The deep life lessons I have learned since I simply opened my mind, and the new places it has taken me is impossible to describe, but I was inspired to capture my personal thoughts as I continue to move through my discovery of "more to life."

I'll be honest. During the writings in the last half of this book, I felt as if I was off the planet for a couple of years (without physically dying), spinning around, and then finally plopped back down in completely new territory. I don't think it would have had to have been this dramatic and chaotic, but I think I was refusing to let go of things I thought were SO critical for the first 50 years of my life. I know now, they were no longer important to me and it was time to let them go. I have also learned to be okay with my sometimes slow learning, since I am here to experience a human life, and my flaws help me to learn sometimes. We really are perfectly designed with all the tools we could ever possibly need, right within ourselves and within our experiences.

So here are the articles I was inspired to publish for the first 5 years after releasing RISE ABOVE THE SH**! Now, one couldn't possibly put everything they learn in 5 years into a single book, and I'm also hoping to add short video clips to the AnniePress.com website, so look there if you want more at some point. I also continue to work on several other projects and will provide links to those as well, on AnniePress.com.

The book is laid out similar to my first book, with short chapters you are meant to chew on a while, until you feel like you're doing it naturally. It doesn't have to be read in order, though you'll share my journey and growth as you see things evolve, if you do. We've provided two listings of the chapters, one grouped by topic, should you prefer to focus more on a certain part of your life, and the second is in chronological order.

As always, you can just open the book to any page that interests you too, for a little quick inspiration, possibly on just what you need at the moment. I still use my books that way!

If you gain one thing that improves your life from this, it was worth the time you spent reading it, and worth the energy I've put into this. So, read on, and try out a new viewpoint, or if it's just not for you, leave it and make your own determinations. But for sure, take the pieces you think you could try and give it a whirl. My hopes are that my learning experiences can move you along faster to your awareness of what an amazing being you are, and to help you start realizing how incredibly capable you are of anything, once you just start trusting that you are here to leave a beautiful mark on the world, in your own perfectly unique way, and that no one else can possibly fill that spot, in any shape or form.

The world is truly counting on you to simply be your happiest, truest, most blissful self. Take advantage of 5 years of my describing how I grew since I was somehow given the courage and first released my words to the world, something I never dreamed I'd ever be comfortable doing. And because of that one little thought, "There has to be more to life than this," I can assure you, I have learned how to live my dreams, and I know with all my heart, it is critical to me, to you, and to the entire world, that you learn how to live yours, too. Much love on your journey. Enjoy the adventure; it is why you are here!

TWO OF THE MOST CONSIDERATE GIFTS YOU CAN GIVE THIS HOLIDAY SEASON

Relationships  ***November 2010***

Hustle, bustle, toil and tussle! It's that time of year again…ALREADY! Sure doesn't feel like it around here, with the warm temps we've been enjoying. Ah, but one of these days, we're gonna wake up, and winter will be here, in ALL its wonder. (Do you have your boots, blanket, gloves, and most importantly, your ice scraper, in your car yet?)

All the same, the holidays are fast approaching and it's time to get going on those Christmas gifts! Sadly, the first thing that comes to my mind is how crabby people get, just before Christmas. Christmas Spirit my #*%! It's more like Spirit Suckers, don't you think? And remember, I try my best to be a "positive thinker!" But maybe if I admit that's what's going on, I can focus on changing it a little…maybe even start a domino effect out there.

You must know what I mean. First, there's the rude drivers that seem to think the roads belong exclusively to them; they're automatically annoyed if anyone else is even on the road. Then, oh boy, if you should get in front of them, or be in the lane they want to switch in to, watch out! You will get a horn, a dirty look, and maybe even worse! Did they all take their angry pill before they left home? Are they just pissed off at Christmas, or what? One of my best friends summed it up and broadcasted one day and said she'd like to tell them, "You need to read this book, dumb#*%!" (She was referring to RISE ABOVE THE SH**!) Cuz we all know, they don't even know why they're so miserable…

Next, you find a parking spot and manage to get into the store without getting run over by one of these people, only to find most of the shoppers and clerks have also taken their angry pill. Don't you dare utter a word to them! I don't care if you need assistance, I don't care if you just want to brighten a shopper's day, YOU ARE NOT ALLOWED TO SPEAK! Ah, whatever! They can kiss my butt!

Christmas is made for us to STOP and APPRECIATE all we have. First and foremost, that means PEOPLE! The people in our lives, the people we come in contact with, and the people that provide the gifts, decorations, and food that we buy. What about the people working crappy hours around the holidays, to make things more convenient for us to pick up things, last minute? I, for one, respect them a great deal…you know darn well there's somewhere better they could be!

Now I know full well that we have an over-abundance of crabby, rude, and disrespectful people running around, so really, please, please, don't ever add to it! Especially this time of year! Even one less "major downer" could make a difference to someone, after all? So, that's the first gift I'm asking you to give…BE NICE!! Spread Christmas Cheer wherever and whenever you can! Please? Start immediately! Not only can you completely change someone else's day for the better, you will also change YOURS! (That's the best part :)

Share a quick smile, an appreciative or complimenting comment, and a little more patience and gratitude and respect. Help out family and friends however you can; they may be under pressure, thinking everyone's holiday joy rests on them and their preparations. Remember and visit or invite in the lonely ones. Many nursing home residents have no one coming to see them. And on those days when you feel like you're not quite up to the challenge, fine yourself and make yourself give extra funds or volunteer time to one of those wonderful organizations that deserve that dollar that you really can afford! Maybe it'll make you think twice next time and it'll still make you feel like you did SOMETHING that day.

It takes so little to turn it around. Can you think of a better gift you can give? Remember, when you start a spark somewhere, it can grow and spread to other people more easily, and before you know it, there's a blanket of warmth driving out the crabbiness! Even if it's just your crabbiness! Try it out this year and see the peaceful difference it makes in your heart.

The second gift can't hold a candle to all that, but it's still very caring and thoughtful. Give meaningful and useful gifts this season, like a book that can help someone realize and start living their dreams, no matter what they've been through. (Hint, Hint) Pamper someone with the things they love when they are relaxing, and put some good reading right in the middle of it. We are meant to learn and grow, and what better "material" gift than something that can change someone's life for the better?

Warmest Wishes for a Full Heart through the Holidays and Always, and GEEZ! Let's be nice out there!
~Mary Anne

MAKE THIS YEAR THE BEST YEAR OF YOUR LIFE !

Self-Love

January 2011

STEP 1 – CLEAN HOUSE

Within reason, get rid of anything and anybody that is not making a positive effect on you, your life, and those in your life. If it's not making a positive impact, it's most likely making a negative impact, which keeps you from the things you want and from being the person you really want to be. The process of "weeding out" can be very simple by just looking at the facts. Consider how it is, most of the time with this thing or person. If it's positive less than half the time, it would do you good to let it/them go. Ask yourself, for the majority of the time:

- Is it/he/she good for you? Is it/he/she good for your health, mind, and soul?
- Do you feel uplifted by this person or thing, or do they or it drag you through the gutter?
- Do you learn and grow by it, or is it stifling you?

STEP 2 – QUIET TIME

Give yourself quiet time. Make a few minutes every day (or at least every couple of days) just for you to talk to you. No TV, no radio, no phone, no computer, or any outside noise. Just you with you.

Think of 3 things you are grateful for and then, tell yourself one perfect thing you would like in your day and imagine how it would make you feel. Believe in it and really allow yourself to enjoy the satisfaction, contentment, and thankfulness of having it. Your positive feelings will open doors you never thought possible. If you really want it, pray for it!

STEP 3 – MORE YOU

Think about and do at least one thing a week that makes you be a better person – a kinder, gentler, healthier, wiser, more effective you! When you give to yourself in this way, you automatically give to the world, at the same time.

STEP 4 – GRAB ON

Grab onto your dreams with both hands! **Dreams are for TODAY**, *not never*, where most people put them! You can change who you are and how you live at any moment in time. Why are you holding yourself back? The world needs you NOW. The world needs you to go after your dreams and be the real you! Stop hiding; it's time to come out and give the world the REAL YOU!

There's no limit to the good stuff, and there's nothing keeping you from making this year the best year of your life. You deserve this; the world deserves this! There's also nothing stopping you, come next year, from topping this year too, once you let yourself start living the life you really want to! *~Mary Anne*

GIVE 'EM WHAT THEY REALLY DESERVE THIS VALENTINE'S!

Relationships 

January 2011

Just how much do you love the special people in your life—a little, or a lot? Think about it for a second. If you love them a lot, then the time of year to show them is NOW! Love is meant to be SAVORED, so start savoring and make it Valentine's Season! I mean, what IF you never got another chance to show them how much they mean to you? Don't you want them to know how you feel? Well then, what are you waiting for?

The thing is, it's so easy, you should kick yourself for not getting on your white horse sooner—but hey—your loved ones will still take it now, no matter how long it took you to come around. So, on to what I'm babbling about. Here are my 2 suggestions for the best you can give, to anyone you love:

1. Give MORE YOU. Give a BETTER YOU. **YOU** are probably the most precious and important thing in the lives of those close to you! So do you realize that the quality of your life and your happiness has a direct impact on those around you, especially those nearest you? Do you understand that if you're not operating at your 100% best, real, and unique you, you cannot possibly give as much to the people that really deserve the best you? Whatever your feeling on your life, it is automatically spilling over to those

around you; that is a fact, and there's nothing you can do about it! Do you want only good things for them? Then give it to them by doing your best to have good things for you!

So, are you taking a little time each week to enhance your life, conquer your fears, take care of yourself, remove negativity, and move towards your dreams? If you are not, you are not only cheating yourself, but your loved ones too! So get started, right now—it's SO easy! Just read a page or two of RISE ABOVE THE SH**! every day or so, and you'll have enough simple ideas for things you can do immediately to make your head spin! Do it for them—they love you dearly!

2. Take the time to put a little thought into a gesture or gift for your loved ones…don't they deserve it? The THOUGHT that goes into a gift this time of year goes much farther than the item itself, and you will receive far more back from them than you ever expected! Pay close attention to comments and wishes of someone you love, and think about what this person really likes. You can make it simple, or go all-out! Here's some ideas in putting together a gift that includes the things they love, or the things they love to do:

    - Take the time to pick up their favorite food or candy or drink item(s)
    - Get a gift card for where they like to go with their friends or for things they like to do when they have time for themselves, or a favorite store they buy things for themselves at
    - Pick out a day or night and follow through on playing with the kids and/or handling other

responsibilities so they can go shopping, to the spa, or out with friends, or whatever else they like doing, but don't get enough time for

- If time with you is what they're wanting, tell them you'll make all the arrangements for reservations, babysitters, etc. so it's no work for them, and go someplace they really enjoy
- Maybe even fill up a box or basket with these things, and other things to pamper them—like a good book on how to go after their dreams ;) Why not? Don't they deserve the world?

No matter what options you go with this Valentine's, make it a SEASON of LOVE . . . they are probably one of the things that really make your life worthwhile, so they should always be your priority in life. It takes so little to show them, and they will appreciate everything you put into yourself and into the gift or gesture for the special day. So really give from your heart, then sit back and embrace the wonderful, unlimited feelings real love brings!

Continue spreading the love of the season on anyone you care about. Hand-make cutout heart valentines or pick up some of those kiddie valentines and give them to your friends and family. You can even tape a small, wrapped candy or trinket to the envelope. I promise, it'll make 'em smile! My friends have told me that opening one of these in the mail made them giggle! (And that's what it's all about!) Show your love, every chance you get. It's what makes the world ROCK! Have a warm-from-the-inside Valentine's! ~*Mary Anne*

LUCK HAS VERY LITTLE TO DO WITH WHERE YOUR LIFE IS!

Awareness 

February 2011

Your life. Your contentment. What's luck got to do with it? Not much, honestly. Are you coasting through life and letting it "GO" wherever it goes? If so, are you completely happy, sitting in the back seat (or maybe even the trunk!), never knowing where you're going or when the next stop is? Wouldn't you rather be driving? Wouldn't you feel a little more in control, if you were driving? *And if you're not driving, who is?* It's kind of a scary, stressful mode to be in, if you ask me.

You see, you really ARE driving, *but chances are, you are throwing so many destinations at your GPS at once, that it doesn't know where to go*. Your most prominent and consistent thoughts, no matter what they are, give your life directions. **Good or bad**, directly related to you, or about something or someone else, THEY'RE ALL DIRECTIONS. Your life decides what to do and where to go, based on the things you think about and believe in the most, but will also stop at rest areas, here and there, based on the rest of your random thoughts!

The MAIN SUBJECT of what you think about the most BECOMES YOUR LIFE. I'll stress the <u>main subject</u> again as helping words, like "I don't want…" are ignored. For instance, if you think, "I don't want to be late," LATE is the main subject and so, you will likely be late. Instead, think, "I will arrive early," to keep the positive, desired thought in your head, instead of what you don't want.

Changing the way you think, and changing what you think about WILL CHANGE YOUR LIFE. Everyone is born with the power of free will and this is what controls your life. My first book, **RISE ABOVE THE SH**! Down-to-earth thinking from Wisconsin**, is a product of some of my life-long dreams, that evolved once I started retraining my brain to focus more on what I want in my life.

Here's another way of looking at it. Each day, when you wake up, you can plan out "your trip" for the day by just taking one simple minute to think about all the perfect things that could occur today and how you and everyone around you would feel, enjoying the perfect moments of your perfect day. NEVER think of the detours or traffic jams, or the negative things, that could occur. Only think about and talk about the perfect route for the day. **Know and believe that day is already yours** and just see what a difference it makes! That's ROUTE A for your day, and if you need help retraining yourself (like I do) to focus on this, I've loaded up ideas on what works for me in the **RISE ABOVE THE SH**!** book.

Unfortunately, most of us don't choose Route A everyday; sadly, most of us choose Route B, most of the time! ROUTE B is when you have all of your thoughts—good or bad—just parked in a big and congested parking lot (your brain). When you wake up and start moving without providing a route for the day, your GPS has to randomly start drawing from any and all of the various thoughts, scattered around in your parking lot. How does it know what to select? Most likely, it'll gravitate towards the main topics of what you are thinking about or worrying about the most, and try to take you to that destination. Distractions or a change in your thoughts causes the GPS to re-route, either temporarily or permanently, and there's no limit to how many times this can occur in a day. If you exhaust yourself with stress, worry, or any consistent, negative topics, your GPS will drive you right into potholes, rough roads, detours, road blocks, and possibly even a crash! It's not the GPS' fault…it's the driver's fault!

So you see, IT'S NOT LUCK that decides where your life goes and how content or fulfilled you are. IT'S YOU THAT DECIDES. So how do you want your life to be? Do you want to travel through life on Route A or on Route B?

Remind yourself of a few critical things, each day, before you decide . . .

1. Route A = Awesome Ride / Route B = Bumpy Ride
2. The world is affected by your presence on ANY "road." There are even some that require your guidance to find their Route A.
3. Anyone near you is forced to ride along with you.
4. You will find more of the real you along Route A.
5. There are no do-overs in life.

Irish Blessings for life-long travels along Route A!
~Mary Anne

THE WHOLE WORLD IS RENEWING ITSELF – YOU SHOULD BE, TOO!

Awareness *March 2011*

(Yep, this is probably the only time I'm gonna tell you to jump on the bandwagon, so take advantage of this!) Ahhhhhh…we made it through another winter, and we know what comes next! The drab gray will soon be replaced with a beautiful green base, and a breath-taking blue topper! In between, everything will come out of its slumber and start to grow beautiful things. New lives will begin, and the beauty and peace surrounds you so snuggly, that you can't help but smile with content. All is as it should be.

So are YOU, as YOU should be? If you've been slumbering and wallowing in the drab all these months (or years), are you ready to wake up and grow too? Look at the proof around you! It's only NATURAL to renew and grow! Going against what's natural here will make you miserable, so stop fighting it and let the **REAL YOU** emerge!

Step 1 doesn't have to be dramatic. It can be just a simple choice that you want something more…that you want something better. Start by making a small commitment, here and there, that you're going to make better choices for yourself, and surround yourself with better people, better options, and ***less negativity***. Any little thing you do will help you to feel better about yourself, and more confident about what you do and don't want in your life. As you gain confidence and practice making positive choices for yourself, you will naturally move towards a more positive life. Work on removing one bad habit, one negative person, one negative influence/environment, or one choice that doesn't make you feel good long term, and just take a moment to notice how much better you feel about yourself!

That's all it takes to get started. It doesn't have to be a huge, life-changing, tiresome effort. It can be whatever pace you want, and as gradual as you are comfortable with. You are in charge. You call the shots. I have to warn you though; once you see the good that it brings you, you will be tempted to pick up the pace and make bigger changes, to the extent that others may notice. This is a good thing, though, as it'll help you identify your true friends. They'll be the ones patting you on the back and encouraging you. They'll be the ones that aren't threatened by the changes that are good for you. These are the friends you should keep, so it's a bonus item!

Then, when you start waking up, eager to have a wonderful day and feel like singing with the birds, DO IT! **Stop the battle where you're your own worst enemy, holding your life back, and JOIN NATURE!**

Don't know how to start? Look up one of the ideas in the 50-some chapters of RISE ABOVE THE SH**! Down-to-earth thinking from Wisconsin. Instead of dragging your life through the muck at the bottom, cheating not only yourself, but the world around you as well, learn to exist in that wonderful world between the gorgeous green and beautiful blue that were **PUT THERE FOR YOU. Rise above, my friend, rise above!** *~Mary Anne*

TO ALL YOU WONDERFUL, LOVING MOMS . . . WHERE DO YOU DRAW YOUR LINES?

Self-Love  **May 2011**

I am positive that one of the biggest challenges a parent has is guessing where to draw the line between how much we give our children and what is ultimately best for them, as far as their development into a responsible, content adult. Too much spoils and stunts personal growth and confidence. Too little threatens self-worth and leaves the parent feeling guilty. Constant monitoring is required to analyze what you are doing and how it is possibly affecting your child's future. So lovingly, we go forth the entire life of our offspring, trying to keep what's best for them in mind.

At the same time, we mustn't lose sight of what's best for us. I want to remind you that you can only do your best for others when you, yourself, are at your best. As a parent, it is critical to the rearing of your child that you pay close attention to the line between giving to your family, and doing what is best for your own personal growth. If you neglect your own personal growth, you not only set a poor example for your family, but you compromise your ability to do what's best for them.

So, to be the best Mom, you have to be the best you. Take care of yourself, in every area…health (sleep too!), your relationships, your dreams, your spirituality. Mind, Body, and Soul.

Taking all of this into consideration, let me ask you something. If you could make a wish right now to get what you need most today, what would it be? As a mother myself, I know what I have consistently wished for …more time and more energy! Now as I explain in my book, RISE ABOVE THE SH***!, we DO have the power to bring about our desires, and this is an easy one, believe it or not. I'd like to share what I do to get more time and energy; as always make whatever adjustments you need to, to do what works best for you.

STEP 1: This is the MOST IMPORTANT STEP! Pick out a start date (how about today?) and figure out a couple of ways that you can get to bed a little earlier. You may need to forego something you're used to doing late at night, so it may be habit-changing time. SHUT EVERYTHING OFF! The computer, the cell phone, the TV. EVERYTHING! Better yet, shut them off earlier in the day and start a new general rule in your house as to when they can be on. I always made my kids earn screen time by doing a chore for every half-hour they wanted. They were happy to do the chores and felt proud to help, it made a HUGE difference getting the housework done, and there's little argument when it's time to shut things off! So, when it's bedtime, try your best to get EVERYONE in bed at a reasonable time so that the whole house is quiet and you can all lay down to a peaceful environment to drift off to sleep.

STEP 2: Once you're in bed, with it nice and quiet, spend just a minute to think about the next day, in the order of events, and see pictures of how it would be, if it were absolutely perfect. What would be happening?

How would you feel? See all the smiles and don't allow any non-perfect thoughts in. You will get what you focus on, so why not make it perfect? Why would anyone think about a non-perfect day and therefore, ASK for a less-than-perfect day? It's a waste of time and a waste of life, so I emphasize, think only about a PERFECT day coming up! See it, believe it, and make it happen.

STEP 3: Waking up and jumping right into work isn't any fun, but waking up, excited to be doing something for yourself is AWESOME, so why not do that? Set your alarm for just a little earlier, to allow for something new you want to do in the morning. (It'll help you peel yourself off the pillow in the morning, too!) Adjust your wake-up time according to what you want to get done, but maybe not all at once…just a little earlier at a time may help you succeed faster. I STRONGLY RECOMMEND that when you first wake up, you jump into some kind of exercise, IMMEDIATELY, before you have a chance to distract yourself. THIS IS THE KEY that sets everything else in motion, so please, please try it! A few important things about this:

A. It must be fun, relaxing, and easy on your body or you will not do it! What do you need the most? What would you like to try? Here's some ideas: Exercise shows or videos (including dance!), fitness magazine workouts, walking (my favorite) alone or with a neighbor or family member, gym workouts or classes, or catching up on reading while using a stationary machine. Think BIG on this and do something fun!
B. DO NOT OVER-DO IT, or you'll want to quit! The right exercise should not hurt! Take it at your own pace, work up to your goals, and stretch out properly

during and after. Let yourself warm up to it and let your body get used to it. Do something different every day, if you want!

C. Hydration and nutrition matter! Anything you eat is your fuel, so make it good. ALWAYS drink plenty of plain water, all day, and especially right when you wake up—you haven't given your body water for probably 8 hours, so it's thirsty! Thirst and muscle cramps are signs that you are already dehydrated.

D. Music or a book to listen to will trigger the brain to help the body. It's not just a distraction; the right type of music will actually give you more energy by triggering certain chemicals in the brain!

E. ANYTHING YOU DO HELPS! Even 10 minutes of stretching or walking is better than nothing! Any time you move your muscles, you are helping your body, inside and out! I truly believe that whatever exercise time I give myself first thing in the morning stays with me ALL DAY . . . it supplies extra energy in direct relation to the exercise effort. You'll probably banish the afternoon groggies for good, and firm up faster like I do, when I work out in the morning! It's a great thing!

F. Even if you want this early morning time to catch up on something else, you can do that too. Just exercise FIRST, then use whatever extra time you have to get a jump on something else. When you do both BEFORE your old, normal daily routine, you'll feel like you've got the challenging world in the palm of your hand! Take a moment to notice the gorgeous, peaceful sun rising; it all feels so good!

G. As you exercise, allow the extra clear head you have to think through and plan out your day, again, visualizing only a perfect day; that's ultimately what you want, after all, isn't it? Staying flexible is also very important, as we don't always know the exact method that will be used to grant us our desires. (More on this in the near future.) I also use this time for my prayers, both for myself and others.

After this, you won't need any more of my steps, because you'll find that the clear head, extra energy, and knowing you're taking care of yourself will automatically help you take care of the rest of your day, and better care of yourself. You wanna be the best Mom you can be? Then you HAVE to be the best YOU you can be first! It all comes from the very core of your being, so you can't ignore what you need most and then expect to be good at the rest of your life! Take care of yourself and it will automatically help you take care of the rest of your world. You may even be so inclined as to start in on some of those dreams you've been holding back all your life. Why not make this Mother's Day huge? :) Love to all you deserving Moms! *~Mary Anne*

WHY DO PEOPLE LET US DOWN? MAYBE, TO TEACH US?

Relationships  ***May 2011***

For the most part, I've learned that negative feelings like being angry, upset, hurt, sad, depressed, or vengeful are such a waste of time. In addition, it transforms me into something I'm not. It makes me ugly, unproductive, and usually regretful, as I push something I really wanted away from me. I say, "I've learned for the most part" because here I sit, writing this at 3am on a Saturday morning, without a wink of sleep on one of the rare days I have a chance to sleep in. Hardly productive. Hardly what I wanted for myself today. Yet, I am learning. . .

About 10 hours ago, I felt hurt and let-down by someone I care about. At that very moment, my highly-productive week came to a dead stop. All my rushing around and extra efforts to prepare for a "perfect weekend" have me exhausted and confused, as I have done absolutely nothing since then besides veg-out, tear-up occasionally, and finally, force myself to think through the positive reasons why this might be happening. It wouldn't take me so long to let myself look for the positive reasons, if I'd give up the pity party of feeling hurt…in my case, it only took me 10 hours, today!

So I think I finally know why. I went into yesterday already exhausted—exhausted from putting what everyone else around me needed, before even thinking about what I needed or wanted, all week. I made assumptions that if I took care of everything else, it'd put me in a position where I could take care of me and my needs. Then, one person's change of plans blew my whole plan apart. I recall very quickly now, that when we don't do what's best for us, we automatically affect those around us in a negative way. **It's never just about me; it's never just about you. Everything we do has an effect on the rest of the world.** Even if you isolate yourself, you're still affecting someone by what you're not doing, but should be. I've been negatively affected by both what this person is doing AND by my failure to myself. And now my unproductive, off-course behavior is having a negative effect on the person I care about as well. I have a mess that I have to try to explain to this other person. I have a mess that I need to turn around for myself, to keep from feeling further disappointment in myself. Thank you, God, for the sleepless night that is forcing me to do something about it before the weekend's over. I realize You were here all along, trying to help me understand; You were simply waiting for me to want to look for it, as You never force anything on us. Thank You for that beautiful gift of free will . . . even on days like this, where I'm my own worst enemy. . . I think? :)

I'm thinking it's all very simple and wouldn't have taken me 10 hours to come up with, had I not coated it in so much junk and over-thinking to start with. I'm pretty sure this can all be prevented in the future by doing a couple very basic things: 1) Communicate better with this person; 2) Don't make assumptions about what the other person is planning; 3) Encourage the other person to do what is best for them more often;

and 4) Keep what's best for me in the mix of what I'm spending my efforts on.

Again, I realize that if either one of us had kept better sites on what we wanted for ourselves, the situation would never have happened. Both of us are to blame for letting a crazy-busy and chaotic week interfere with what we really wanted. I am responsible only for myself; I have no claim to being upset with this other person, as they are only human, too. It reminds me to be a little more understanding of others that let me down in any way. It's probably not what they set out to do, rather, it's probably just the effect I'm feeling, from them not taking better care of themselves and going after what makes them truly happy, deep down and long term. My job at this point, is to climb out of my self-pity pit and take a good look at the big, open world around me, and go back to what I know will make me feel proud, content, and productive with my time, once again; and the sooner, the better. Once I do this and have a clear head, I need to communicate unemotional facts to the other person, as to what I'd like in the future, to keep this situation from occurring again.

While this very simple thing works for my situation today, realize that there are times when some people neglect their own needs to the point where they almost always have a negative effect on you. When it's this extreme, you have to decide what's best for you, even to the point of distancing yourself from them, either temporarily or permanently. (More in my book, RISE ABOVE, on that.)

For those of you who have read my book, I want to point out an important fact in all of this. I have NOT spent any time in the last couple of days focusing on what my perfect day would be, which I am adamant about doing, so I take full responsibility for where I'm at. I left it to random fate, or perhaps, I even brought it on myself, getting stressed out about getting everything done so I wouldn't be where I am now, on my precious weekend. I gave more focus to where I didn't want to be, than on what I wanted, so I know, it's my own dumb fault. There I go, being all human again! Might as well use those distractions, short-comings, and mistakes to keep learning and growing! ;)

Warmest wishes that my hard lesson has a positive effect on you, somehow! *~Mary Anne*

HOW TO GET THE MATE OF YOUR DREAMS

Relationships  ***June 2011***

Finding the mate that's perfect for you does not have to be as difficult as most of us make it. After 20 years of relationships, I finally tried something new, and it absolutely brought me the mate of my dreams. While none of us is perfect, he is absolutely perfect for me, and it's absolutely nothing I've ever had before. I wish everyone could experience love like this, so I want to share what I did to change this part of my life.

I don't know if it's the romantic, fairy-tale fantasy or the fear of being responsible for our life, or a bunch of other stuff, but it doesn't matter. For some reason, we tend to sit back and wait for that perfect someone instead of making things happen. We need to be clear about what we want in our life, appreciate it, and go after it. As always, it all starts with you, and it's all things you should be doing for yourself anyway, so you've got nothing to lose and oh, so much to gain. I'll get right to it!

1. I TRAINED myself to STOP any thoughts about bad memories with guys...to only let myself think about the fun and the things they did that made feel great. I try to think about the nice things they did or the laughs that we shared, even from the really bad boyfriends I had. (The bad thoughts do only harm to

you.) This doesn't make you want to be with them again, because you know they caused you more harm than good and that relationship is supposed to be over. What it does is remind you that someone knew you were deserving of that kind of treatment, and remind you how wonderful you felt.

2. Along with that, I thought about my DREAM MAN...how incredible and real and kind he would be, and how incredible he would treat me, just because he loves me just exactly for the way that I am, but also always supporting me to grow and to be a better person. I thought a little about physical attributes, but more so, about his character. We need to be very clear on what that perfect person would be like and KNOW that person is out there.
3. See yourself with this awesome person, doing things you'd love to do with them, how it feels being together, and being grateful for how awesome your life is, and how awesome you feel, even when you're not side-by-side. BE GRATEFUL in advance and know you will appreciate and respect this person as much as they do you. Now if you have values or things you want this person to share with you, take the time NOW to be more active in those types of activities yourself. I know many people that have met their spouse this way. Look for groups that meet in person or chat over the internet regarding a common interest. For instance, I've noticed there are Catholic Singles and other religious outings, all kinds of classes, activities, and Meetup.com groups that are specific to certain interests or hobbies. Look around, indulge yourself and have a ball!
4. DREAM BIG and be the best person you can be in the rest of your life, knowing that you want to be clear-headed and ready and happy with your life so that when this person drops into your life, you will

show them your best side and they will have no doubts that your life is a happy place to be, and know that's where they want to be. Get rid of any self-doubts and baggage and scars from anything in your past before this person comes along, so they want to dive in once they get to know you.

5. SMILE, SMILE, SMILE and keep your life FULL of things to smile about and appreciate every day, which is just another chance to make your life great! I thank God every day and this makes me more content than I've ever been. Ever.
6. Remember, outside influences like the news, listening to other people talk, and songs and TV makes you think about whatever you're seeing/hearing. Distance yourself from, or learn to quickly ignore negative communications that do not coincide with the thoughts you are trying to focus on. Learn to quickly switch to a thought that you wanted, versus thinking about the negative or contrary images. THIS IS SO IMPORTANT! Learn to surround yourself with only positive, caring people and events. If it's not good for you, don't do it! Your time—and your life—is worth so much more than that!

Want more ideas? There's lots more in my book, **RISE ABOVE THE SH**! Down-to-earth thinking from Wisconsin**. How long will it take? That's up to you and how aggressively you do these things and how firmly you focus on it and believe. For me, I met someone within DAYS of starting all this. I soon realized that he was what I was wishing for, but that after I had it and saw the outcome, I wanted to change my mind and redefine a couple of things I really didn't want. I got more specific and didn't waste time dating anyone that didn't provide a wonderfully positive and happy environment for the both of us. I spent a lot of time working on me and my dreams and was honestly very content with that, knowing I'd have lots to offer when my perfect match showed up.

He did, too, less than a few months later, ONCE I WAS READY. Because I was ready, I constantly reminded myself to keep my heart open and real, so that love could come in. This is great stuff, believe me! Don't hold yourself back from it. Also, you should know, you can use the same principles to get your dream career, other relationships, and even perfect day, after perfect day. Go for it! *~Mary Anne*

ENEMIES? HIT 'EM HARD . . . WITH LOVE AND COMPASSION!

Relationships

July 2011

Life is NOT about comparing yourself to others. It's NOT about being better, knowing more, or having more. There is no reward in your heart, or in anyone else's heart for achieving (or thinking you're achieving) these things. True love from someone does NOT come from these things. True love for yourself does NOT come from these things!

Life IS about how you treat others, and how you treat others has a direct impact on your happiness and fulfillment in life. As a wise man I once knew said, "It's nice to be popular, but it's more popular to be nice!"

Think for a moment about the people that annoy you. Do they seem to be on a mission to prove they're better, they have more, or they know more, by chance? See what I mean? Now, going along with my concept of it having a direct impact on their happiness and fulfillment, do you think that person is overjoyed with their life? There's a good chance they're not. There's a good chance they could use some extra divine help, whether they think they do or not.

So my solution for people that aggravate you? RISE ABOVE, of course. First off, do NOT let them alter the way you want to behave in any way! If you do, you lose. It never makes you feel good, long term, to descend down into the crappy way some people treat each other sometimes! So even though I know this (and wrote many chapters on how to rise above, in RISE ABOVE THE SH**! Down-to-earth thinking from Wisconsin), I was still struggling with not letting this type of people get a rise out of me!

Then, I received some major "good help" during a recent mass I attended at the Shrine of Our Lady of Good Help in New Franken, Wisconsin **(www.shrineofourladyofgoodhelp.com).** The homily that day was on loving your enemies and praying for those who persecute you. Though I've heard this, my whole life, it never sunk in, till I heard it there. I also kept hearing my girlfriend Teresa's words throughout the day, "All that matters is love and compassion." She has had her deceased husband tell her this, over and over...

The priest was saying that of course, it's easy to pray for and love those that are good to us. The challenge is with those that are not so good to us. The love side tells us that while we do not have to accept or even try to understand what they do, we do need to pray for them all we can and forgive them all we can. We need to realize that most likely, they don't know what they do. I do find it easier myself to feel sorry for them and apply the compassion side of it. Then, as we make the sacrifice and pray for them instead of wasting the time being angry or worse, we HEAL ourselves. **He said it is the ONLY WAY TO HEAL OURSELVES.**

It makes sense, and I do feel better myself as I say a quick prayer for these people every day. It seems that magically, overnight, these people seemed to stop the nasty behavior, at least, towards me. It also seems to be helping me get over it and to not harbor resentment, which I really struggle with! It just seems to be fading away. I am hopeful that even if that person aggravates me again, it won't bother me as much, and I will be able to deal with it with a much more level head and steady emotions, which makes me feel good about myself.

I also better understand the "healing ourselves" part of it because coincidentally, I've been listening to some personal growth interviews, where I discovered that a lot of what I still do to hold myself back, comes from sadness or anger in something that someone else "did to me" at some point, which of course, tends to make me angry! So I've been working through this myself by praying for these particular people and praying that I can completely let go of these negative feelings and create NEW possibilities for myself. I am fed up settling for the limitations I used to automatically apply to myself, thinking I had no choice, but I know better now, that I AM choosing. I'm choosing to HEAL MYSELF through praying for my "enemies," and it's amazing to see the power it has!

Once again, try it, because you know you've got nothing to lose! **Happy Healing!** *~Mary Anne*

ALONE IS NOT A BAD THING

Self-Love

July 2011

Why do we associate being alone as a bad thing? Is it from childhood time-outs that we received or gave, and now we relate alone time as being "bad," like no one wants to be around us? Time-outs aren't to teach us no one likes us, yet I think that's the part we remember. The purpose of a time-out is to get the offender to stop, be quiet, and think. Once we stop and think, we remember who we are and how we should behave. (Wish we could freely hand out time-outs to adults we see misbehaving!) So anyway, don't misinterpret time-outs or time alone as thinking you're bad and no one likes you; remember that it's just to help you stop and think. We all need time to think.

It's okay to be alone. No, not forever, since the whole reason we're here is to interact with each other. But temporarily and routinely, alone is a good thing. Throughout our whole life, we experience separations from those we care about. Death, physical moves, divorce, and the like separate us permanently from someone we were very close to. Children growing up, temporary trips, and relationship changes can also seemingly take someone away that we care about. We don't want to be left alone. Even with more minor separations, like job or other relationship changes, we feel a loss and possibly alone.

It's okay. Alone is good. It'll be okay. Alone allows you to breathe, to think, and to learn more who you are. When you find yourself alone, don't drown yourself out with constant electronic device activity! Tune in to yourself! With all the noise and chaos sometimes, tuning into yourself is like finding that little radio station sandwiched in between the overpowering ones, but it's the best station there is, so it's worth the extra effort.

QUIET is GOOD. We all need quiet at some point each day to hear ourselves think. THINK! Don't be afraid to think! It's a very, very good thing. It's a great thing! It's the only thing that will lead you to peace. Peace is within, and you can't possibly hear it with all the commotion you probably have going on. Life changes constantly. It attempts to prepare you to learn more about yourself and what is best for you. If you don't let yourself go quiet, you can't hear it. Quiet is good. Quiet is the key. Alone time is the easiest time to find quiet.

People don't abandon you. People love you. We are all here to love each other. The fullest love for others can only be achieved once we love ourselves. The stronger our love for ourselves, the stronger we can love and assist others. We learn how to love ourselves during that quiet, alone time. So quiet is good. Alone has its purpose. Let the purpose come. Let the purpose grow you. It is time for you to grow. Realize this is why you are alone at times. Learn to allow the growth! Make good use of the alone time so that when people are in your life, you can best serve them and help them grow. I've packed thought after thought about why we and others behave the way we do and how to change it, in the book, RISE ABOVE THE SH**! Down-to-earth thinking from Wisconsin. After that, when you're ready for some divine help in your purpose, I highly recommend the book, **Angelspeake**, by Barbara Mark and Trudy Giswold.

New chapters in your life are constantly beginning, which simply means the chapter before it must end. This is neither good nor bad—it is simply just life moving forward as it needs to, to help you grow. Move forward. Grow. Do not sit at the end of a finished chapter. Move on to the next and embrace it. Learn. Grow. Love yourself and others. More chapters will come. More life will come. Do not be afraid. It is just life.

Just as life has chapter after chapter, so do you. Are you the same exact person you were 10 years ago? Even 5 years ago? Of course not! You are constantly growing, learning, and changing. Yes, you have some chapters about who you were behind you, but that is different from the current chapter about who you are now. The chapters about who you will be have not yet come. Again, don't sit at the end of a finished chapter. Allow yourself to evolve as you naturally should and continue on to the next chapter. It's all a very awesome adventure. Aren't you excited to see who else you are and what else you are capable of? You will be amazed. You deserve that alone time to continue writing the chapters about who you are.

So your alone time is there to get to know yourself better. That way, when you're around others, you can give them the REAL YOU. That's all people truly want from each other. . . REAL. Who wouldn't want to know you? You are really something. You are astounding, and have gifts to offer that NO ONE ELSE HAS! Every single life has an incredible purpose that no one else can fulfill. If you think anything less of yourself, it's just because you don't really know yourself that well yet. It's okay. You'll learn. Take the quiet time to learn and grow so you can really share what you have with others, especially when you meet someone new. Be ready to show them the **REAL YOU! Keep learning about the real you—the adventure goes on, your whole life!**

P.S.-Even if you are not feeling separation at this time, don't you think it'd be a good idea to make some routine alone time for yourself, anyway? That is, unless you already know how incredible and amazing you are and realize you can accomplish absolutely anything. In that case, you may be well acquainted with the real you already. :)

Have a blast getting to know you. You will be impressed! *~Mary Anne*

TAKE BACK CONTROL!

Awareness  *September 2011*

So I haven't written a note in quite a while! Sure, I've been busy, but I can't use that as an excuse. After all, if we truly want to do something bad enough we will make time for it, somehow. I have a prime example in how I wrote the majority of RISE ABOVE THE SH**! Down-to-earth thinking from Wisconsin in the middle of the night. So I reminded myself today that something wasn't quite right; something was stifling my writing inspiration.

With everything I've been doing the last couple of months, my energy levels aren't exactly stellar right now, though I can't complain because everything on my schedule is very fun, and completely my choice. I just realized that the gloomy weather and lack of energy that everybody's probably feeling right now seems to expose us more to negativity--negativity that I could nip and kick to the curb quite easily on a good day. There's probably more grumbling and more less-than-helpful comments floating around right now too, because most everybody's in the same boat. The pile tends to grow, when we keep adding to it!

So I know where it's coming from, and even though I know how to keep the SH** from sticking to me, there it is, plastered all around me and keeping me from one of my most fulfilling activities. Come to think of it, it's keeping me from a few of my favorite activities, including just laughing with people I love to hang out with. And if it's keeping me from some of the things I love doing the most, what toll is it having on my day-to-day routine stuff? **Are we all being choked to death sometimes, when we can't keep our heads above the seeping pool of negativity that's been quietly rising around us?** That's what negativity does, after all. Negativity sucks you away from what you really want, and makes you miserable and tired, in mind, body, and soul.

It's not right, you know…having negativity from other people, events, and things suffocate our day and our life! Think about it. **When we're too occupied with all that negative crap, including people that aggravate us, and painful past memories, we are NOT taking the time to be the person we REALLY want to be and to be living the kind of life we REALLY want to be living.** We are letting it rob us blind! So we have to stop and remember, that no matter what is going on around us, we are STILL THE BOSS of ourselves and our lives. I, for one, am ready to resume control!

The biggest, baddest defenses you can throw at negativity are your feelings. Use them! Stop and think for a minute after the people contact, the event, the activity, the thought, whatever it may be…stop and think! How do you feel? How do you feel an hour later about it? A day later? Does it make you smile? Does it make your heart feel warm? If not, it's likely stifling you and your life, so why waste your time on it? Wouldn't you rather be spending your time on what you deserve…being happy and reaching for your dreams?

Any time you spend on something that leaves you less than joyous robs you of the time that happiness

should be there! Any people contact that leaves you feeling uncomfortable in any way is telling you they're not allowing you to be the real you! **Discomfort and discontent are there to scream at you, "This isn't for you! This isn't who you are!"** Pay attention! There are only so many hours in the day. There are only so many hours in your life! So ask yourself, what kind of life do I want? A miserable life? A so-so life? Or do I truly want the life I was born for—to live my dreams and to be incredibly happy?

I recommend you try something a little different today and be amazed at how easy it is, how great you feel, and how it was always right there, at your fingertips! You call the shots with what you spend your time on. Don't allow negative anything to consume you! Choose wisely. **Replace any negative thought, person, or activity with something that makes you feel good and positive.** Pray for people, pray for what you need, appreciate what you learned from it and what you have and how you have grown. Think only about your ideal life and what you want in it, and how the ideal you (the REAL YOU) would act and feel.

TAKE BACK YOUR DAY! TAKE BACK YOUR LIFE! Not only are you impacting your life with every move you make, but everyone around you as well. You are not alone in this world, so there's no way around it. Do it for you…do it for the world. It IS that big. YOU ARE THAT BIG! Find happy. It's sitting right there, patiently waiting for you! Overjoyed to be writing again! *~Mary Anne*

THE TERROR OF CHANGE!

Change  ***October 2011***

CHANGE! Does the very word and thought of it give you the shivers and scare you half to death? Well, you're not alone. In fact, most of us hate change so much that:

- We cling to bad relationships, like there's not one single other relationship out there to have. Sadly, a bad relationship keeps us from getting into the good relationships we SHOULD have, including the good, confident relationship we should have in loving ourselves.
- We cling to jobs and lifestyles we hate, and don't even start looking for other jobs or training or learning that could help us get another job. We think we can only do one thing at a time. Really? Says who?
- We think we have to live the way we do to cope with people or things in our life and we're afraid that changing something will make us incapable of that in some way. I hate to tell you, but when you're doing something that doesn't really make you happy, just to be able to "deal with" something or someone, it's just a matter of time before you realize you no longer want to live that way and that you need to change it. Do yourself a favor and don't wait for things to get ugly and miserable. Small changes can surprise you and make a big

difference, and make things better for EVERYONE. Never be afraid to listen to your heart and do what you know is best. People that truly love us, LOVE US. Period.

- We close our minds, hearts and very souls against any new or different views, ideas, or learning, literally stopping all growth in any of these areas. Seriously, do we think that we've reached a point where we know it all, or are we just afraid we just might expand our knowledge and desires and have to admit we have been letting silly excuses choke out the dreams and happiness we really want?
- We say, "I'll do it later. . . or . . . some day." Exactly why do you want to seal yourself in a tomb until then? Exactly why do you want today to suck? There are no guarantees that you'll get tomorrow.
- We say, "But I've never done it before and I don't know how." Silly! How come we encourage AND EXPECT children to TRY new and difficult things (walk, talk, and learn constantly), but we think it's just fine for us to sit on our butts and not take the chance of trying new things? What is wrong with us? The only way to know if you can do something is to try, and even if you don't succeed 100%, it still feels like a success, because you tried! You might even try it again, learn and succeed at it, eventually! You KNOW there are things you always wanted to look into more, or to try. YOU KNOW IT! So what the heck are you waiting for? You have no idea of what you are capable of until you try it.

Do you feel my frustration? Do you feel yours? Hey, that's good, because frustration is the first step in getting excited about CHANGE and SEE IT FOR THE

HOPEFUL THING IT REALLY IS! What's the very worst that could happen, anyway? You get your hopes up and if it doesn't work out, you'll be wounded forever in some way for trying? But you know what? That hardly ever happens unless you go into it with your mind set on failing. When you are set on failing, you don't really try and then even if you begin to succeed, you purposely make it fail. Why do we do this to ourselves when we know anything is better than where we're at?

Deep down in your heart, you may really want it, but then you let the lies of your ego tell you, you shouldn't, you can't, or you don't deserve it! Accordingly, you let the evil part of your mind have full control over sabotaging everything about it. You don't even try to stop it and then you let it rub your nose in it and tell you, "See, I told you, you couldn't do it!" You let the lies of fear and self-doubt take control when you allow this!

How do you know when it's the truth in your heart talking or the lies of your ego and fears talking? Easy! Ask yourself ***how you feel*** when you have these thoughts. If you feel icky, undeserving, sad, or restrained, it's the evil lies of the ego challenging you. On the opposite end, thinking about something that makes your heart jump or dream, makes you happy or excited, **is the truth and your rightful path**. **Listening even just a little to how you feel** helps you stay on the smooth, easy, sunny road in life. But when we let the fears of our ego detour us, we usually end up having to work our way through a difficult terrain of potholes, bumps, and even closed roads, where we have to back up and turn around many times and take the long, hard way through life, never knowing what's up ahead! To me, that's way scarier and unsettling than embracing changes!

So on days when your life sucks, how do you feel about it? Based on those icky feelings, you now know that it's the lies controlling all of this. Now that you realize it's a big fat lie, let me remind you that you being here is not "random." There are no "extra people" in this world. We are all here for a very good reason and in order for the world to function as it should, each one of us is necessary. **Any one person that goes after the life of joy they dream of automatically helps the world along.** Any one person that doesn't go after the life they dream of hinders the world's progress. You are not alone. You are meant to live an incredibly happy, fulfilling life and that, in turn, benefits the world. **You are more important than you know**. Change is hopeful. Change is exciting, not scary. Only the lies are scary. Truthful thoughts warm your heart, to let you know it's the truth. Welcome the truth in. Welcome change. The world needs you.

So take back the wheel. Hasn't your ego detoured your life long enough? Force your ego into the back seat and if at any time you hear it being a "back seat driver," simply tell it, **"Yea? Well I'm driving here, so just sit back and be quiet! You're distracting me from going where I really want to go!"** If you ignore it long enough, it might just fall asleep back there as you're cruising the smooth roads and leave you alone for a while. And if bumps in the road wake it up and it starts jabbing at you again, continue making changes to fill your car with new riders that will help you hush it up quickly.

Any time you do the slightest thing that makes you smile or learn or allow yourself to try something new, you invite these good riders along to travel with you. Fill your life with good people and good things. If you like this analogy and want to use it literally to remind yourself daily, get an inspirational audio book like RISE ABOVE THE SH**! Down-to-earth thinking from Wisconsin and listen whenever you're in your car. Trust me, it drowns out the lies of the ego, fears, and self-doubt in no time!

Thank you for sticking in here with me. It proves you do want more for yourself, so stop being silly and welcome change into your life. I have a little homework for you now:

1. Share just one of the ideas from this article (or the whole article) with someone that might appreciate it.
2. Look at one unhappy thing in your life and just let yourself think about how you really want things to be and then do something! Go through all the options you have to make either a tiny or a huge change—it's always your call. You can try a bunch of things—there's no rules or barriers here besides the ones you set up.

Warmest wishes for your new, hopeful, exciting, changing adventures! *~Mary Anne*

COLOUR MY WORLD . . .

AND YOURS

Awareness 

November 2011

Remember that old song, by Chicago, that goes something like, "As time goes on, I realize just what you mean to me. And now, now that you're near, promise your love, that I've waited to share. And dream of our moments together. Colour My World with hopes of loving you…?"

If you look outside today and you aren't completely amazed by the blazing colors out there, let me suggest that you adjust your internal vision. **They say that the more open and loving your mind, body, and soul are, the more vivid the colors of nature will be to you.** So what is it that makes the colors more brilliant? What keeps your mind, body, and soul open? That's easy. It's the single, most important thing in your life. It's the single most important thing in the world, that's all.

PEOPLE. People close to you. People far from you. All the people in between. You see, we were given each other to serve the most important purpose in life. **Each and every person we come in contact with is there to help teach US a little more about who we are and what we are here for**. Without others, it is impossible to learn this. Good or bad, happy or sad, brief encounters or life-long relationships, it's all there to help

US. The disappointing truth is, most of the time, we miss this important opportunity. We don't take the time to acknowledge the people around us and we completely miss the chance to learn more about ourselves—our REAL selves.

Think of it this way: You are always surrounded by the mural called life. There's always a million beautiful things going on, all around us. **Our internal vision and our free will chooses WHAT to look at**. Most often, unfortunately, we pinpoint one little tiny piece of the mural, it appears to be dull, and we and miss out on the "bigger picture." Other times, perhaps, we are more open-minded, and look at a larger chunk of it and things are more vivid and easier to understand. But if we are wise and treat others with the respect and appreciation that they deserve, we are able to see a large section, or even a whole side of the mural at once. Life is beautiful, everywhere we turn. We are seeing a lot more of what's REALLY there.

Can you imagine the breath-taking view we have, when we are kind, compassionate, and giving to others? Can you understand why some people choose to live their life this way, serving others? I mean, not only do they wake up to an amazing world outside, but they start to see an amazing world inside themselves as well. You've heard me say that anytime you give something, you receive so much more back. The receiving channels of that are too many to get into here, so again, I'll single out one of the biggest things we get back. **When we give, we grow.** We learn something more about ourselves and clarify our life, as we wipe some of the smudges off of our internal vision. Then, automatically, the viewing areas grow larger.

The best part is, giving respect and appreciation to others is so incredible easy. Eye contact, a smile, courteous driving, saying “Thank You” to the person serving you in any way, being generous with a tip or donation, taking the time to listen to ANYONE that is reaching out to you, be it someone close to you or a complete stranger…oh my gosh, it is SO easy. **It actually requires more energy and difficulty to be rude, and it’s much harder on YOU, so why bother?**

And how about your loved ones? Come on! What are you waiting for? Do you tell them every day, how much you love them? Remember how important this is by understanding the simple fact that they could be gone tomorrow! Thank them, every day, for something you appreciate about them. They probably have no idea how amazing they are, just has you have no idea how amazing you are. As the weather turns colder, let’s heat it up, inside and out! Wait until you “SEE” the real you…you’re gonna like YOU!

Colour someone else’s world now, and just watch what is does to yours! ~*Mary Anne*

'TIS THE SEASON OF PEACE. WHY NOT LET IT IN?

Self-Love  ***December 2011***

Regardless of your beliefs, there's one common theme that rings loud and clear at Christmas Time. LOVE. God LOVES YOU. God reminds us at Christmas that each and every one of us is so important and critical to the world, that He sent His Son to be with us, to remind us of this. None of us is an "extra." Each and every single one of us is here for a reason. We ALL have a purpose. If you give that just a little thought, LOVE comes easy. Love for others, and more importantly, love for yourself!

We forget this so easily and seem to need to be reminded constantly. Let it sink in during this opportune time of the year! Let the incredible peace of the season snuggle you tight! Do you know what that feels like? Have you ever let it happen? If you HAVE let it happen, you KNOW how amazing and secure it feels. There is no mistake, and it's something you long to feel again and again; on top of that, it's something you long to have others experience as well…so you do your best to share this with them.

If you are not able to get to this wonderful place, ask yourself what you are waiting for. Do you feel like you don't know how to get there, or that perhaps you don't deserve it? Let me make some suggestions. First, the deserving part. Listen to me! God tells us over and over and over again that He loves us and only wants us to be happy. He doesn't say, "If you're good, you deserve to be happy, but if you're not, you don't!" That's our silly, warped thinking that goes there. God wants us to be happy and to feel peace, so that we can find our true selves, discover our gifts, and share them with the world. It's just a natural thing, and if we start to love ourselves, we naturally are good to ourselves and others, and that leads to more awareness of who we REALLY are. Focusing on what really makes us happy and at peace automatically brings everything else…so step over the silly excuse that you don't deserve it and just remember, you have to be your best to give your best to the world…peace is part of the best you.

Now, about how to get there. Start with just thinking about what you're doing every day. Are you filling your day and your brain with electronic noise, distractions, and pointless things that are NOT helping you find peace? Are you numb to your feelings and your thinking? Are you allowing negativity to hang around? Are you in a robotic, suppression mode? Why? Why are you so mean to yourself? You can't possibly hear your heart through all of this! STOP! Get rid of the noise, especially the TV. What GOOD is it doing you anyway? Is it teaching you to love yourself more? Doubtful. Try your daily routine and holiday tasks WITHOUT a TV, radio, cell phone, computer…none of it. Even just for a little while. Ask yourself, "What would I really like to do to let my REAL self out a little? What can I do to remove something negative in my life? What would bring me peace and fulfillment? What really makes my heart skip?" Then, LISTEN. Listen to your heart, and your heart only. You know when it's your heart when it feels warm, happy, confident, and excited. You know when it is NOT your heart talking when it's critical, judgmental, mean, negative, hopeless, or icky in any way. (That's the lies of our warped fears from the areas of our real self that we've been neglecting. We are suffocating certain parts of ourselves that really need to be let out. Instead, we let the bully that's holding them hostage talk, and we listen to them! So STOP!) Listen to your poor, MUFFLED heart that's trying so desperately to be heard through all of this noise pollution! Turn away from the noise, inside and out!

Then, DO SOMETHING DIFFERENT! Do something your heart wants to do! Whether it's stopping self-destructive habits and actions or finally taking the time to do something that will make you feel great, it doesn't matter. (Idea: Share the joy of volunteering or giving with your family or friends!) Start SOMEWHERE! This is the perfect time of the year to start this!

Don't even try to tell me you can't find the time…that is a silly excuse the bully inside you makes up! Seriously, cut out an hour or two of TV and use that time to get something done, so you do have the time! Find a church or service and take yourself and your family. Oh my, ESPECIALLY YOUR KIDS! SHOULDN'T YOU BE TEACHING THEM HOW TO FIND PEACE? Isn't that the most important job you have as a parent? If you don't teach them, who will?) Just GO! Go, sit, and experience about an hour of peace. Let your kids look at the beautiful decorations and nativity scenes. EXPLAIN to them that God loves them more than anything, and so He sent Jesus to teach us how to love, and that is what we celebrate this time of year. LOVE. Get rid of all your silly excuses and just go. Your kids will remember, and no matter what, they will make their own choices as they get older. You want them to have a strong base for making those choices, don't you? You want them to know how important they are to God and to the world, don't you? It will make you feel GOOD as you remember, God wants this for you. God wants this for every single person. If you don't know this by now, LET yourself go to services and LEARN.

Life will inevitably be rough at times, but if you just remember that God is always there with you, you will feel the peace. You don't have to know how to get there; you only need to want it and to allow it. Learn alongside your children; let them help you find it again…they are much more open and less tainted than we are. :) Learn together. Your heart will feel full knowing you helped them learn how to find peace, no matter what, especially during the majority of their life when you can't be next to them. God=Good. God=Peace. Let yourself learn and grow and experience this, and you'll never go back to your "noisy world."

Snuggle Yourself & Your Loved Ones in Peace this Season and ***Merry CHRISTmas***! *~Mary Anne*

HURTFUL WORDS HURT YOU THE MOST

Difficult Situations 

December 2011

Whew Boy! All the wonderful gatherings we have this time of year can be so wonderful to catch up with everyone; we feel obligated to fill the time together with any kind of chatter. So it gets really easy to throw in the latest gossip. We have to be careful here, as WE FORGET HOW MUCH IT HURTS ALL OF US! I know that if we stopped to think about this first, we'd keep the focus on ourselves instead of the others that are not there to defend themselves.

Let me give you a visual to consider before you think, type, or utter any negative words. Picture bad thoughts as a DAGGER IN YOUR HAND. When you decide to engage in thoughts or words that are not helpful to anyone, you raise the dagger high overhead and viciously stab it into the person or persons you are talking about. It doesn't matter if what you are saying is true, false, or speculation…the jabs occur whenever you pass along or think of anything that does not directly benefit all involved.

But that's not the worst of it. Your dagger stabs everyone else in the vicinity as well, including whomever you're communicating with and anyone they communicate it to, and so on, and so on. Still, it doesn't end there. Gossip is a rampage of emotional harm to all.

If that troubled couple you're talking about has children, you're stabbing them too, along with anyone else associated with them. THE DAMAGE YOU CAUSE IS IMMEASURABLE!

But there's more. The negativity of your stabbing spree TURNS THE DAGGER ON YOU, AS WELL. The last blows are to yourself, and they continue as the destructive force you initiated continues through other people, intentional or not. Your only hope is in the wise choice by others, not to partake in the mass destruction, or in prayers sent up to counteract it by anyone, including you.

Let's think about why we select negative communications over positive, helpful ones for a moment. Well, we are only human, aren't we? But, we still have to remember, we are in full control of our thoughts, actions, and especially, our communications. There's only one reason we chose to point out flaws in others…it's because we are unhappy or fearful of something IN OURSELVES. Perhaps we are not truly comfortable with who we are, and deep down, are afraid others will see we're not perfect, and so, we try to distract them with the faults of others. Maybe it's because we know we are not all we should be, and we try to convince ourselves "we're better than someone else" by putting their weaknesses on display. Are we accomplishing this? No. We really do know better.

First of all, we KNOW that icky words from us leave us feeling icky. We may try to deny it, but we know full well, it is NOT making us happy. We KNOW it doesn't make ANYONE happy, and so WE KNOW we are the source of someone's hurt and sadness. That does NOT feel good! We do ourselves the most harm, as it drives us further and further away from loving ourselves and others, from finding our true selves and our dreams and fulfillment in our lives. Everything we think, do, and say has one of two effects: It either helps us realize better who we really are, or it drives us away from this. There is no in between.

Likewise, as we do things that are good for us, we automatically have a positive effect on others, but when we do things that harm us, we automatically harm others. Again, there is no in between, as much as we want to deny it. All we have to do before we type or speak is to think, "Is what I'm going to say going to help, encourage, and inspire myself and others? Will it make me feel happy and proud forever?" If the answer is NO, then DON'T DO IT! STOP THE MADNESS! You won't regret it and don't worry about people thinking "you're not in the know!" Truly, WHO CARES? Wouldn't you rather have people know they can trust you and that you're better than that? So think about it…

So hey, I know how easy it is to partake, and I have to actively work on keeping my head clear in an attempt not to get sucked into it. A couple of things that work for me:

1. Distance yourself from people and situations where this routinely occurs.
2. When gossip occurs, attempt to change the subject, walk away, or try to end it by politely indicating the facts about how everyone has to live their own life or that your talking about it doesn't help, and how you'd rather talk about things that really matter in your lives.

3. Pray for strength and courage in always having a positive effect on others, and pray for the speaker and all affected by it. There is tremendous power in prayer!
4. Keep your life focused on what is good for you and what makes you feel blissful in life; it's also a great role model to others. Truly, we need to spend more time working on ourselves, versus others. Everyone has the right to choose their own life and their own actions, even if we truly believe they are doing something wrong, it's still their right; we have no authority over them (unless you are the parent of a minor, of course). Lead by example, give your honest advice if they ask, and hope they see and want to imitate your good qualities, eventually.
5. As I research the very real energies that are proven to exist, I see a trend where electronics and closed-in environments tend to "pen-in" and increase the negative energies, but nature, animals, and natural light (sun, moon, and stars) tend to "absorb" and remove negative energies and feed us positive energies. Just try weaning yourself off of any of your electronics more and getting outside more, and just see how you feel after that! I've read that we should all get outside for at least an hour a day for this very reason…just try it and see what happens! There's also a favorite saying that I read once, that comes to mind whenever I'm outside looking around, that goes something like this…"Even the majestic trees and humble blades of grass reach for God and the heavens, as we should…"

Let's show a little more love to others and ourselves as we step into the New Year! If you have any other ideas on warding off negativity, please post them to my Facebook wall. Simply go to my website, AnniePress.com and click on the FB symbol to get there. God bless you as you make this coming year the BEST YEAR OF YOUR LIFE! *~Mary Anne*

LOVE YOU

Self-Love  ***January 2012***

LOVE really is ALL that matters and ALL you ever really need in life. Absolutely everything in life revolves around it, and is dependent on the level of love there is. Think about it! Oh, there are many kinds of love, through many kinds of relationships, but the one that is REQUIRED in order to have any of the others is the most simple of them all.

It's the one that you control completely, entirely on your own, and it, in turn, controls your life and your level of contentment in life. **SELF LOVE is the ROOT of your life**! Your level of self-love calls all the shots:

- How you treat others and whether you can give and receive love
- Whether you are happy with your life
- What kind of people and situations you allow in your life and whether they can harm you (we only allow things to harm us up to the point that we're willing to harm ourselves; our own cruelness convinces us we deserve to be treated badly!)
- Whether you pursue your dreams or not
- TRULY, whether you are currently living in heaven or in hell

So this is easy; **if you're not overjoyed with your current status, you could use a little (or a lot) more**

self-love. It really is the only thing that can help you and help your life; it is the core of your existence and there's just no getting around it! Again, love may come to you from other sources, but unless you love yourself completely first, you can only deflect some or all of it…you can't absorb all of it, nor can you give others what they deserve…you can only give out what you, yourself possess.

Even if we've lived our whole life so far with a tremendous lack of self-love, it's NEVER TOO LATE! There's a very quick way to that self-love. Simply be the REAL YOU. The challenge for most of us is figuring out who we really are and then, to break through all the lies we live by and start allowing the truth to lead us. Just by the little I know about myself at this point, I'm sure learning all about who I really am will be a life-long adventure! Learning one thing leads to another, and another, and another. It's an absolute blast!

I just finished an interesting book called, The Four Agreements, by Don Miguel Ruiz, and he describes our fears, self-doubts, hurts, and lies as "… a parasite that controls the mind and controls the brain. The food for the parasite is the negative emotions that come from fear. If we look at the description of a parasite, we find that a parasite is a living being that lives off of other living beings, sucking their energy without any useful contribution in return, and hurting their host little by little."

I can't think of a better description! It's dead on, as it silently kills you and your life! **There is only one way to kill the parasites, or the lies and fears and hurts and self-doubts in our hearts, and that's to start**

being our REAL SELF! Even if we have no idea who that is, or how to do it, we can learn IMMEDIATELY! It's SO easy and SO fulfilling, I want you to promise me first that you will not be angry with yourself for not doing this sooner! Promise me that from this point forward, you will let go of old habits and simply love yourself for the wonderful, unique person you are, and ACCEPT that you DO YOUR BEST! Promise? Okay then, on to HOW TO BE YOUR REAL SELF!

LISTEN TO YOUR HEART! LISTEN TO YOUR TRUE FEELINGS! This may take a little practice because we are all so in the habit of letting the parasites drown out the real feelings of our heart, but if we're very honest and quiet with ourselves, we WILL hear the truth!

Start with this: In EVERYTHING you think, do, or say, ask yourself, **"How does this make me FEEL?" Then, here's the key…**

<u>If it warms your heart</u> (yes, physically) and makes you feel happy, peaceful, excited, proud, connected to God and the world, or any of the deep, lasting, positive emotions we have, it's your heart and your TRUE SELF TALKING! It's an incredible feeling that you'll long for, once you get a taste of it, which makes it very easy to follow the path to your dreams and fulfillment in life.

On the other hand, if something you think, do, or say makes you feel unhappy, undeserving, anxious, upset, unimportant, fearful, or icky in any way, it's coming from the lies and the parasites! It is the DIRECT OPPOSITE OF LOVE—both love for yourself and love for others, and it is NOT THE REAL YOU and NOT SUPPOSED TO BE IN YOUR LIFE!

Yes, it's that easy…just let yourself try it and just watch the wonderful things and people that come into your life! I recently recorded a speech I gave on the importance of each and every one of us, as we all have a strong impact on the entire world. **If you'd like a few more ideas in finding your true self, you can listen to it on our website, AnniePress.com.** (As always, there are no strings attached, so share away and make someone's day!)

Just wait till you start getting to know the REAL YOU. I guarantee it, **you're gonna love YOU!** ~Mary Anne

ARE YOU PICKING YOUR/THEIR POISON?

Health  ***February 2012***

Want to hear a very real and scary statistic? **One of out of two people will have a serious health condition.** YES! You have a 50% chance of getting seriously, even deathly ill! Bet you know a few people that have deadly diseases right now. It's time we wake up, people! We are doing this to ourselves, and it's SO unnecessary! It's SO EASY to be healthy…why do we seem to want to die young? With endless food and drink options, we pick the ones that contain POISON (toxins) ! Seriously, do we have a death wish or just like to take risks? I've pondered the excuses…

1. It hasn't killed me yet. Sure, maybe it'll take a while for the dose of poison to get built-up enough to start making you sick, but have no doubt, it IS taking its toll on you. Bet you're not 100% healthy and energetic all the time, and bet you're increasing your odds of being the 1 of 2 that get sick! **So you like risking your life, huh?**

2. They can't sell stuff that's unsafe, so they can't prove it's poison. Really? Come on, WE KNOW

BETTER! First, there's all the uncontrolled imported ingredients that have NO regulations (look at the big apple juice articles recently) and second, just tell me you've never, ever heard of a product that was sold or used in products for years, and later pulled because of lawsuits of people dying or permanently ill! Isn't it more common to hear about unsafe things these days? You know there is supporting research behind those claims, and it has to be really bad to even be leaked to the public! Even our recent, local news had these comments from the experts in both the research and government fields: **There's no way the FDA can regulate everything that's in the products we consume. They only have to list the main ingredients, and it's nearly impossible to test for everything. In food alone, there can be over 77,000 pesticides used. Peeling an apple does not eliminate the exposure to the chemical. The chemical goes all the way through.** This makes total sense to me, since everything is porous. Just like our skin absorbs everything and allows it to go into our body, so does food absorb anything from the outside. (Our skin absorbs all the chemicals from soaps, shampoos, makeup, cleaners—even chemicals left behind after our washed clothes or floors or counters are dry. Make no mistake, that stuff ends up in ALL our bodies…this includes our children!)

3. I like it and can't live without it. Bet you can. Bet you can find something else to replace it, that you

may even like better and that gives you more of whatever you're looking for, like energy or satisfying your thirst or taste buds. Anymore, we have an unbelievable amount of replacement options; there's just no excuse! **Fact is, YOU WON'T LIVE AS LONG WITH THE TOXIC THING!**

4. Other options are too expensive. Hate to bring you into the current decade, but with more and more supply of other choices, you will usually find something better, safer, and healthier at the same price or even less now. Look around! **There's so many places to buy safe and healthy stuff anymore!**

5. It's a hassle to change now. Are you saying that you and your loved ones are not worth the time or brief thought it would take to try something different? Maybe you don't think your life has any value then? I gotta tell you, you're dead wrong about that! You ARE HERE FOR A REASON, and **your health affects people close to you, people you work with, and even society in general!** Is it fair to knowingly create a burden for others? There are all kinds of convenient, cost-effective online stores too. Allergies are disappearing at my house since I've switched!

6. I'm going to die anyway. No kidding. Even if you feel like you've fulfilled all of your life-long dreams

and you're ready to leave this life, as long as you're stuck here, don't you want to feel good? Even as we age, what most people are afraid of is thinking old equals sick and unhealthy. But I'm trying to remind you, growing older will be whatever you make it! Yes, if you don't pay attention to your health, your reality of getting older will be feeling sick. **But that's your choice. It is possible to age and STILL be healthy, active, and energetic. Really, that's how it's supposed to be.** And here's a horrible thought: What if you really don't care right now when you die, but next year, you realize you have a lot to live for and want to be healthy, but you've already killed your body beyond repair? That would really bite!

7. It runs in my family…my genetics are going to make me sick anyway. Oh, whatever! You know that we ALL have potential killers living in our body, our whole life. **We also have bodyguards. Every choice we make feeds one or the other**. Antioxidants will even kill the poisons. Why would anyone chose to feed the killers? But, it's what we are doing, with the non-healthy choices we make…we are FEEDING THE KILLERS! Again, seriously, WHY?

Obviously, there's more to our health than just the one drink or food choice we make, but this is an easy place to start. I'll be writing a lot more about the other health factors, of which, nearly all of us are very aware of, and again, just choose the killer options. It's so sad to me, as I watch all the people around me struggle with life-threatening diseases and chronic aches and pains…and I cringe when they think that modern medicine is their only hope. The truth is, medicine and surgery only takes care of 10% of the health problems out there. 10%!! **God bless the doctors out there, for keeping us alive when we're in a bind, but we need to realize that they're not miracle-workers and they have no control over the health choices we make.** It is a guessing game for them, as they have no knowledge of what you have done to your body all these years, and that is what the medicine is dependent on.

Health is the ultimate cure…the medicines may just give you a few more days to make better decisions, but not always. : (On a more positive note, I just read that someone, somewhere, has recovered from every type of cancer that is out there. It doesn't have to be terminal, even when the medical doctor tells you it is. I personally know people that have proven the doctors wrong, here, but remember, the doctors can only try to control around 10%. The rest is completely up to us!

RISE ABOVE THE SH**! Down-to-earth thinking from Wisconsin has a couple of chapters on health, and lists of things that are known to be toxic to our health…things like the #1 killer, stress, and to never using plastic in the microwave. Changing to something safer, like glass, is so simple! This is so easy, and it could be the one thing that keeps you from getting cancer or many other health problems!

So, decide if you're going to continue to pick your poison or make a simple, convenient change to something safer. Yes, it is your life, but remember, your choices always affect EVERYONE around you, especially those that love you. You can ignore all of this and continue taking in all those unnecessary poisons and risks, but then if you get sick, remember, THE BODY IS MADE to renew cells and to fight off all the junk we put in it. **All we have to do is feed the bodyguards instead of the killers.**

If you or a loved one have ANY health aliments, be kind and take a good hard look at all the risks, and at the simple changes you could make to reduce them. Even one small change can help! That is, IF you want to stick around a while and have an active, healthy life. It is always your choice. Here's to your healthy life!
~Mary Anne

LESSONS FROM A SUNNY BEACH

Awareness 

March 2012

If you've been following my theme of learning at all the last couple of months, you know I've been focusing on self-love. Like many, my level of self-love isn't always where it should be. In fact, I had a tremendous lack of it for most of my life…I was just always putting everyone and everything else first. Now I understand that I can only give my best to others when I am at my best and the very core of this is accepting and loving the beautifully unique person we are. It is so necessary to the world's survival that we all honor the simple fact that we are not exactly like someone else, because that would be entirely useless. The world needs EXACTLY what we have to offer, rough life experiences and flaws and all. It's absolutely our own, unique personalities and life experiences that make us perfectly qualified to do our specific missions in this life. How can we even think for a moment, that we are less than significant in this world?

So, following my heart's signals to take a little break from my all-to-common, busy routine, I set up an inexpensive simple vacation to 80-degree weather, finally taking that long-overdue bonding time I wanted with my only daughter. She works a lot of hours now, too, so it was wonderful to watch the stars align and shove us on to the airplane with just a couple weeks' planning. We both knew it was absolutely meant to be. In advance, I envisioned the usual inspiration the beach, ocean, and warm sun was bound to throw at me, but even so, the relaxation and rejuvenation was over the top!

As I first stepped out onto the beach, I spotted a couple of white sea shells and was careful not to step on them, but as I got closer to the water, I realized they were everywhere! It was impossible to walk in or near the water without crushing them. I felt a little guilty at first, destroying such natural beauty, but as I looked around a little more, I was quickly reminded that the gorgeous, soft, white sand came from the very same type of shells I was destroying. Over time, the living creatures occupying the shells no longer needed them and they were now best utilized in another fashion. The glistening white sand was just as wondrous and necessary and amazing as the intricate shells.

The piles of shells lying around different places on the beach reminded me of people. Every morning after the tide washed out, there were colonies of the same type of shell in some areas—almost a hundred of them sometimes—but the very next day, they were usually gone. Sometimes another type of shell group or two would be close to the same place, seemingly because they were allowed to hang out with the main group. Or perhaps the other shells didn't even realize they were different at all. Perhaps they thought they were just like one of the other, more popular shells.

Sometimes the shells seemed to be mostly in perfect condition, but other times, they looked like they had come through a rough ride to the shore, where they ended up in a million pieces. Often, there would be remnants of crabs, sea weed, fish, or sea urchins intertwined. The first day we arrived, I noticed one of our neighbors had what I call angel's wings shells lying outside their door to dry, and I hoped I could find some myself during our stay. I watched for them on the beach for 3 days, but saw none. The next morning as I was taking a quiet, long walk during sunrise, I nearly stepped on some.

As I looked closer at the tiny shells, I found hundreds of them in a pile, in all sizes and colors. It was as if someone gauged my path and dumped them in a neat 2-foot by 2-foot circle that I couldn't miss. The tide had left them behind of course, as most of them were anchored in the sand somehow. As I looked closely and carefully started picking them up, one pair at a time, I discovered there was even more. Lodged in between them, here and there, were a few other very tiny and detailed shells, and as a bonus, some of those little white birds (doves?) that you find in the center of sand dollars! I couldn't believe they were all left behind a few feet on the shore, when the waves should have easily drawn them back in to the ocean!

What a treat! I've learned not to question the everyday miracles and to just enjoy them and to look up and say, "Thank You!" Even now as I'm writing this on the plane home, with my sand and shell treasures in tow, the sun is setting outside the airplane window. The various shades of deep orange are absolutely breathtaking, reminding me that the gorgeous, peaceful sunrises and sunsets of the last few days, go home with me.

We were in Southern Florida, probably in the most friendliest place I've ever been. Absolutely everyone you came across was helpful, happy, and relaxed.

Everybody! This made it one of the most relaxing vacations I've ever taken in my life! Can you imagine this little corner of the world, with no visible stress, anywhere? I credited it to day after beautiful day of full sunshine and nearly 80-degree temps. It really was a mood-setter and begged everyone to be outside, where nature does its magic in filling us with positive energy. Everyone was plump-full!

Oh, but the last day there, we did stumble upon a "pessimist" as my daughter called it. In a group conversation on the trolley, one man piped up and said that while he was a permanent resident with a home only a block from the beach, he hadn't been to the beach in over a year. We all looked at him in bewilderment, hoping he was joking as we waited for justification for this insane behavior. He continued, "I wake up EVERY morning, just wishing the clouds and rain would come in! I'm so sick of sunny days…that's all we get here!" I was too dumbfounded to speak, but a couple others spoke up, saying they were really enjoying the weather, since they were visiting from the colder northern states with snow. "Oh, the snow is why I moved here. I couldn't stand it!" He said.

I don't think any of us understood him at all, and I had to write his comments off to him just not thinking at all about what he was saying, or more so, what it was he really was not liking. He just didn't seem to know what he wanted; he just didn't know any better. We truly have to stop and think about what it is we want in our life, every day, or it becomes too easy to take things for granted, and to start complaining about the very things we really wanted in the first place! I want to hope there's just more to it with this guy, and I said a quick prayer that he can be happy and let himself think clearly about what he really wants in his life. It's a prayer we should send up for ourselves and others at least once a day. I thank God for the reminder and for the perfect vacation. Here's hoping you take a little Spring Break and STAY CLEAR! *~Mary Anne*

ANGELS ARE NOT SCAREY

Awareness  ***April 2012***

Do I believe in angels? Oh my gosh, you have no idea! I seriously don't know where to begin, so I'll just give you highlights in a chronological version. At a very young age, my loving parents took the time to teach me about God and angels…mainly that they are with me at all times…that I'm never alone. The "Angel of God" prayer has brought me and my loved ones safety, comfort, and good outcomes thousands of times, I know, and it's because I ask for a little extra help watching over my kids, when they're not with me. Instead of worry, I simply say a quick prayer or two, and I know it's taken care of.

But I have an advantage, I guess…you see, I KNOW without a doubt, that they are there! Remember that our free will either allows or doesn't allow things in to our life. So in order to have something you really want, you have to ask for it in a positive way, believe, be patient, and be grateful, all at the same time. Stay focused on what you want and never think about what you don't want; you know this from my book, RISE ABOVE THE SH**! Down-to-earth thinking from Wisconsin.

So anyway, I was fortunate enough, that at a very young age, before self-doubt and fear was a part of my life, I saw what a child's simple faith could do. Even before I was old enough to understand, at the age of 8, I wasn't devastated when my 9-year old brother (and best friend) was suddenly not home one morning. He had suffered a great amount from leukemia and truly, I was just happy he was no longer in pain and had gone to a wonderful place. Of course, I started missing him right away, but I think it was Mom that told me to just talk to him…that he was there…so I did. Without delay, I felt his presence and his warm smile, and he told me he would always be with me; all I needed to do was talk to him. The joy I felt from him, as he assured me he was so happy, is indescribable. I talked to him each night for a little while, and slept peacefully with a smile on my face.

You need to understand, there was nothing holding this connection back because at that age, I had no doubt. Without knowing or even thinking about what could happen, I just missed my brother and did it. I just started talking to him. My free will, with full belief, allowed this to happen. Then sadly, as we grow up, and the world gets a hold of us…

The world starts telling us that we have no proof and it's only wishful thinking and dumb luck, and just like anything, when you hear something often enough, it takes some of your focus and puts it on the negative junk you really don't want in your life. Like any weak human, I too have had my periods of negativity and doubt, and a lot of "I don't deserve it" attitude, which again, was a crappy gift from the lies of the outside world. When we listen to the outside world instead of the truth in our hearts, we drown out this beautiful connection; we drown out our real selves. I'll be writing and speaking a lot more on this soon, but I want to get back to angels.

So, here I am now, finally going after my dreams in life, as I've finally realized that heaven is more of a state of being than a place. As I allow all the wonderful things life has in store for each one of us, I constantly venture into new and unchartered territory. At first, this terrifies most people as it did me, but something kept telling me," just keep doing what you're doing," and that "everything you need will come." Scared as I was at first, my inspiration and passion was just stronger (but boy, was I praying a lot!) As I succeeded in one new experience after another, overwhelmed with gratitude for all the additional bonuses that accompanied them, I became less afraid. I started to realize I had some very powerful help keeping everything in line. Feeling more comfortable with having that help, I finally started to acknowledge a number I had seen repeatedly at the peak times of my new career as an author. "222" was showing up everywhere (and still does), during my heavy writing periods. As I was writing my first book, it honestly scared me a little, but I kept hearing a voice, telling me it was a sign and everything was good. As I became busy with the business side of everything and pulled back on the writing, I don't remember seeing the number for many months, but then, when I started going after my dreams again, it started up again!

This time, I had a little more courage and my curiosity finally made me google it. WHOA! The internet told me it was a sign from the angels to keep doing what I'm doing; that I'm on the right path. Well, I couldn't help but read a little more on this, and that opened a whole 'nother world for me. Within months, I had books and more signs and angel authors landing at my feet, to where I seriously needed to pay attention to it to move forward! I know now, this is simply because I was finally allowing my angels to communicate with me; I was finally at the point where my doubt is gone and my will is to have their help more actively. We all have at least a couple of angels assigned to us, patiently waiting and hoping that we please give them something to do! They long to help us to succeed and be happy, but again, our free will calls the shots.

I have to tell you how easy life can be, though, once you let them do their job. Anything from, "What should I wear today?" to "God, keep my loved ones healthy and safe!" is cool…they want to help with EVERYTHING and as you allow it, you can learn how to HEAR THEM, all the time. I'll be writing a lot more about what I've learned about angels in my next book, but I don't want to downplay the times I REALLY knew they were with me, and I could really hear them or see unmistakable signs I had asked for.

It's at our lowest, scariest points of life that they shine their brightest. As God's Messengers, they can perform miracles, and all we have to do is ask, believe, be patient, and be grateful. Even recently, as I grow impatient for the outcome of a new project for teens, "TeensRiseAbove.com" and for a couple of close relationships I have with people I love, I woke up to a loud, clear message. Besides reminding me of all the 111's and 222's I've been seeing all day long, every day recently (which remind me that angels are with me and to keep doing what I'm doing), I heard, "It's just not ready yet! It will be soon, so be patient. You know you want it to be the best it can be, before you move forward. It's coming, it's just not quite ready yet!" Thank you angels; can't imagine where I'd be without you! *~Mary Anne*

STRUGGLES? COME OUT OF YOUR COCOON!

Change  ***May 2012***

If I promise not to be a major downer, can I talk to you about something that absolutely breaks my heart, every time? This upsets me so much, I'm having a hard time finding the words to describe it at the moment, so bear with me.

Please, someone, help me find that "sure way" to wake people up from the hypnotic struggle they chose to exist in! Yes, we all are free to choose how to live our life, but throwing it away shamelessly hurts SO many people around us, near and far.

I know where it comes from. Someone or something pushed hurt or fear or wrong information towards somebody else, and now, they're forever stuck in the SH**! Not only do they not know how to find the truth and escape, they seem to find comfort—yes, comfort—in the struggle. They think it's "normal" and that they fit in more when they are struggling! They feel more secure risking it all because it's more familiar to them, and so, they don't even try to step out of the SH**, even as it grows massive enough to choke and kill them or their life.

Again, you may think I'm exaggerating, but give it some thought, and tell me I'm wrong (please!). . .

→ People seek out and choose harmful relationships, pushing good relationships away
→ People choose to risk their health and think it's "normal to be sick, once in a while or even permanently"
→ People mindlessly spend days, even their whole life, in misery and doing things that do not fulfill them

Now I don't take it personally when I tell people that for just 5 minutes of reading a week, my book will absolutely give them ways to make life incredibly happy, and they are not the least bit interested. I respect the fact that not everyone wants to be happy, for reasons I am so blessed not to be able to comprehend, but it still seems impossible for me to sit by quietly and watch someone literally destroy themselves and/or their life.

We've all known of extreme examples, and have probably handed easy solutions to people on a silver platter, only to be ignored until hearts are broken, lives end from disease, and lives end in regret. So sad and so unnecessary! It's heart-wrenching to watch someone literally throw their life away, as they refuse to pause for a moment to consider if it's truly what they want! It's even worse to consider all the other lives they impact in a harmful way, especially their loved ones and children, who are extremely likely to continue the self-destructive patterns they observe! : (

If you know me at all, you know I'll risk overstepping my bounds at the mere chance it may provoke some thought, whether now or any time in the future. It's not always welcome, but I sleep better at night knowing I tried. All the while, I have to remind myself that everyone's free will gives them the right to live however they chose, even to the point of pure misery and destruction of themselves and others. All of us do the best we can, at the time, and we need to pray more for clarity and guidance for ourselves and others.

As we notice someone struggling and try to help them, we need to respect the learning process required to learn that life's lesson. Think of the person struggling as being wrapped up in a cocoon, hiding as it makes them feel safe. We can provide encouragement and advice as to how to emerge from the cocoon and what it will be like to have wings and fly, but we should not pry open the cocoon for them. A real butterfly must go through the slow process of breaking the cocoon open to build the strength required to survive once out of the cocoon, and its wings are not ready immediately. It must rest and be patient while its wings dry out and complete the transformation to prepare them for flying.

It's critical, then, that we not enable self-destructive behavior by catering constant attention or too much help to someone who really isn't ready to come out of the cocoon. Prying it open and pulling them out will cause permanent damage to their wings, possibly making them non-functional. We all know people that will never fly, either by choice or because someone pulled them out of their cocoon (like parents that control and spoil their children, for instance—those children will never even realize they have wings or what they're for). Such a waste, isn't it?

So to anyone I may have offended in my feeble attempts to coax them out of their cocoon, please remember me in your prayers, rather than waste any energy on negative feelings about it; right or wrong in your eyes, I do the best I can, too. And to those that have been my angels, reaching out and providing divine inspiration for my struggles, I can never thank you enough. Wonderful things happen when you simply exist as your true self, like the very talented photographer, Vince Carter, who graciously gifted me with a large photograph of a real butterfly, just as I was pondering my frustration with helping people out of their cocoons. I had not shared that frustration with anyone; there was no way he could have known. I framed that photo and look at it, every day, and it brings me wonderful comfort.

Thanks so much for "listening" today . . . let's do our best to open up our wings and encourage everyone to do the same . . . I truly believe no one really wants to crawl and just drag them behind, their whole life! See you out flying! *~Mary Anne*

ACHIEVE HEALTH BY USING REAL COMMON SENSE

Health  ***June 2012***

Why is health such a mystery these days? Most don't pay any attention to their health and then wonder why they have health issues and then wonder more why medicine doesn't work all the time. Others pay a little attention to it, but believe the general consensus or pick out a small piece of something they heard and never apply their own logical thinking or do any research on it. It seems these people don't really care about their well-being at all. It seems they don't understand they only **have one physical body in this life** and that they're stuck with it, until the day they die, no matter how bad of shape it's in.

Then there are the rest of us, that want to be healthy, active, and happy throughout our entire life. Some of us DO understand that everything we do to our bodies WILL absolutely determine our physical state until the day we die. Some of us DO want to have the best chance at feeling great all our life. Personally, I love learning and proving to myself that even a little effort DOES work. I rarely ever get sick…at all…no matter what is going around, including when I am cleaning up kids' puke for days. Like most of us, I had seasonal allergies for 20 years. **I HAD allergies-they're gone now**. I was to the point where I had moved into the stage of fatigue and body aches, no matter what medicine I tried. I didn't mind the sneezing and congestion; it was the headaches, fatigue, and constant body pain that I couldn't function with.

So just in case you might be interested in what I have proven works to improve health, including maintaining a weight you are comfortable and happy with, read on. My book, RISE ABOVE THE SH**! Down-to-earth thinking from Wisconsin, has a couple of chapters dedicated to health and gives you endless ideas to improve your health, no matter what is going on, but here are some very general and additional things.

Every single body has the ability to ward off disease and repair itself, no matter what hereditary qualities, exposure, or statistics exist. The body is made to detoxify and repair itself. Take one example of allergies. I was allergic to oak pollen, dust mites, and other seasonal things. **Pollen and dust mites have existed forever, yet with each generation, they seem to aggravate more of us**. In my case, it suddenly caused a problem for me in my 20's but now, 20 years later, allergies no longer bother me. The oak pollen and dust mites were a constant throughout, and are obviously still there.

We are SO used to the statistics, we just assume so many people have to get sick from cancers, heart disease, nervous system disorders, allergies, asthma, etc. and that's just how it is. **Why doesn't it seem odd to anyone that we just ACCEPT this thinking and roll over and die when it hits us?** Why doesn't anyone talk about how easily we can prevent and even heal all of these issues, just by not being negligent with our health? Why do so few pursue getting healthy?

Disease is quite simply, almost always caused by negligence of health, period! Removing the negligence nearly always restores health, as you ALLOW your body to follow its natural path of healing itself, with or without medicine. Medicine can only help about 10% of the issues out there, and only temporarily. **The other 90% of your health depends on how you take care of yourself.** Think about all of this…doesn't it make sense to you? Sure, medicine MAY keep you from dying or give you that 2nd, 3rd, 4th, or 5th chance to PAY ATTENTION to your health, but it cannot CURE you. The body itself is truly the only thing that can heal the body, right? How else do you explain the Stage 4 Cancer Survivors?

It's so easy to know if you're taking care of your health. How do you feel, physically? There's your answer. It's so basic! Do you have all the energy you want? Do you rarely get sick? Are you at your preferred weight and fitness level? If you said YES to all of these, your body is happy. But if you answered NO at all, your body is probably being neglected, somewhere. In addition, here are some sure signs your body cannot handle what you're doing to it: swelling, bloating, irregular digestion, congestion, headaches, and really ANY health issues at all. The issues are your body's way of screaming, "I cannot keep up detoxifying and repairing! You are NOT giving me what I need!"

Do you understand, it is NOT NORMAL to feel ill? It is NOT part of aging, it is NOT part of your gene structure…it is only caused by one thing: **Your body is not getting enough of what it needs and is probably getting too much of what poisons it**. Inflammation, anywhere, is your body fighting and screaming that it does not like something. Feeling yucky when you go too long without something (like coffee, sugar, salt, or anything) is your body going through withdrawal! Pay attention to it! I think you can get addicted to just about anything. Your taste buds have been corrupted by the chemicals you've been consuming, but if you start to replace the junk with nutrient-rich food, they will start to return to normal and be able to taste the true flavors of everything you eat and naturally want healthy foods more, and junk food less, and you win!

I'm not just talking about what you eat and drink here…I'm talking about ANYTHING your body absorbs. **Things are absorbed and put INTO your body many other ways too.** People forget that skin is porous and that ANYTHING you touch goes right through your skin, into your body, just as it would soak into a sponge. There's no magic, invisible shield stopping it! Think about this the next time ANYTHING touches your skin. Soap, shampoo, makeup, laundry detergent, cleaners, lotion…most are LOADED with life-threatening chemicals. The same goes for anything you inhale. Strong smell usually means toxins, and fumes DO seep out of closed containers. Even good-smelling things are laced with poisons. I don't think its coincidence that my allergies disappeared as I began to replace brand-name things in my house with better, safe, more cost-effective products; it's helped other family health issues too. There are many companies that focus on this, and basic products off the shelf you can use for a lot of things (like my favorite, organic virgin coconut oil), so truly, you've got nothing to lose just trying something safer. That's where I started, and I'll never go back, now that I see what a huge difference it makes.

Getting back to what you eat and drink. Unlike many years ago, we DO have cost-effective, easy-to-find organic stuff EVERYWHERE, so what's your excuse for not grabbing it, when it's sitting next to the chemically-packed, nutrient-bled, so-so tasting equivalent? All you have to do is look a little, and you'll find it. Even just one or two organic replacements (like potatoes or apples, which are so full of chemicals you can hardly taste the real food!) gives your body nutrients instead of poisons…every single little thing helps! I'm quite frugal, so I typically replace the items that are equal cost-wise; often it's what's in season. But once you taste the difference, you may be willing to pay just a little bit more for wholesome, organic foods. **You may even start to think you are deserving of a happy, healthy, long life, and this is a small price to pay!** You can easily make up the difference by weaning yourself off some of the expensive junk food.

So, a few things that I found really help me stay healthy:

ADDICTIONS can be formed on almost anything. If you start to feel icky at all, when you go too long without a certain food or drink or substance, you ARE addicted to it, to some degree. You probably think its hunger pains, but it usually isn't—true hunger doesn't give you a headache or make you feel light-headed or aggravated, but withdrawal does! For me, it was sugar, which exists in nearly any processed food you eat. I just started reading all labels and try to keep it under 24 grams of sugar a day, which is nearly impossible. Companies DO add things to make you crave it; why wouldn't they want to sell more? You truly will never know all ingredients and whether they're safe. Listen to your body on this!

DRINK lots (a minimum of half your body weight in ounces) of pure, safe water, every day, especially before bed and when you wake up. Anything added to water goes against this—especially sugar, sodium, and caffeine. Soda, alcohol, and energy drinks ARE toxic, no matter how you try to justify it. Compensate by drinking extra plain water anytime you drink any toxins, or anytime you're exposed to them in any form. Your body needs extra help flushing it out.

NUTRIENTS are craved by your body. If you eat what it needs, you will feel satisfied, energetic, and full. You'll have no desire to binge or eat junk. I recently started using a simple method I read about in a book, and even though I do not do this every day, I could see results in just a week's time! I have more energy, I am losing weight, and I am not as hungry and rarely want anything that's bad for me (fried, sugary, or salty foods).

Ready? This is SO simple. First, chew everything you eat until it's liquefied. Then, only when you're hungry, *work your way up* to eating a pound of fruit in the morning (first thing consumed that day is great for you!) and a pound of vegetables in the afternoon and/or as your evening meal (raw is best). Obviously, you wouldn't probably eat the whole pound at once, but depending what it is, you won't hurt anything. I recommend starting with a little, depending on what you are used to, and increasing as you know you aren't throwing your body into digestive shock. No need to be all gassy because you jumped in too fast, to something your body isn't familiar with. Just increase the volume of the food as you know your body is adjusting to it.

Buy things fresh each week and keep the variety interesting and organic, when possible. I try to make sure some of the top nutrient-rich fruits and vegetables are on my list. It really makes a difference. One doctor's list has these listed as the most nutritious food in existence: Kale, Watercress, and Turnip, Collard, or Mustard Greens. Close behind are Brussels Sprouts and my favorites, Bok Choy and Spinach. Also very good are Arugula, Cabbage, Flaxseed, Broccoli, Cauliflower, Romaine, Green Bell Pepper, Onions, Asparagus,

Strawberries, Mushrooms, Tomatoes, Pomegranate, and Oranges, in the order of best first.

Nearly all meat and dairy have more negative impacts than positive, but I'll tell you right now, I love my meat and dairy. The answer? Get as much of the high-nutrient items listed above and fill in a little with the rest. This isn't about deprivation; that never works. It's about eating the high-nutrient things and giving your body what it needs FIRST before adding the less useful foods and drinks. The internet is FULL of recipes for healthy, yummy recipes using these foods, so you could eat it a different way, every day. I just go with what sounds good. I'm on a bok choy oriental salad kick, right now. I can easily eat a pound of bok choy a day and even add bonus items like flax seed or replace the oil in the salad dressing with hemp seed oil, which is one of the best cholesterol-leveling things I have found yet. (By the way, hemp means "non-marijuana" … it will not get you stoned! :)

EMOTIONS often cause us to eat when we are not hungry, so pay attention to when you do this. Stop and ask yourself why you are eating when you're not hungry, and IF that's really what you want to be doing. I have a habit of eating when I'm lonely, bored, anxious, upset, or after I've had some alcohol. Once I realized this, I learned to try to plan ahead. If I think I might be drinking, I try to make sure my stomach's full with a healthy meal before, as I think I eat then to absorb the toxins; that way, I won't order greasy bar food later. If I feel the urge to nibble or binge when I'm not hungry, I reach for sugarless bubblegum instead, or try to find something to keep me busy and away from the food, until I have my emotions under control. If I am feeling negative emotions, I remind myself that eating unnecessarily will only make me feel worse, so why punish myself more? If the gum isn't doing it, I reach for carrots or something I know is good for me, at least. If everything fails, I take the time the next day or two to exercise more and eat as healthy as I can. Again, every little bit helps!

DETOX occurs naturally, whenever the body is not digesting, and overnight is a good time for this, but the more often, the better, right? For this reason, grazing all day is NOT the way to go, and you're not going to starve to death if you cut back a day, here and there, especially if you over-indulged the day before. My Dad always says, "We just don't NEED all that food… especially the junk." At 77, he's kickin' butt and lookin' good, having already beat the odds of his family health history. Try eating healthy meals, two to three times a day, and let your belly empty out, in between. Watch how your tummy goes down, as it's not inflamed constantly and has a chance to catch up detoxifying. You know we are surrounded by toxins, and we are working our detox process overtime. If you can, finish eating at least 3 hours before bedtime. The more time you give it, the better!

Life is a learning process; I'll write more as I discover more about what keeps me healthy. After all, what do we have, without our health? A healthy world is a happy place! *~Mary Anne*

ALL I NEED TO KNOW, I CAN LEARN FROM CHILDREN

Awareness

July 2012

It's not too late for us, and we have wonderful examples, all around us. While on vacation last week, I had the privilege of hanging out with several of my nieces and nephews, and was reminded of the pure joy that life is meant to be. Here are just a few things they helped me remember:

SMILE and GIGGLE without thinking. Just let it happen. Let it out!

PAY ATTENTION to everyone around you. They are a treasure.

HUG whenever the urge arises. It'll make at least one other person smile and remember their worth.

Say I LOVE YOU often. You can never say it too much.

Know that YOU CAN DO ANYTHING.

BE AMAZED by nature. It is miraculous.

LISTEN to others, especially when they ask you to do something.

GET OVER IT, when something doesn't go your way, and quickly. There's something better to do now.

If you are tired and crabby, REMOVE yourself from others until you are willing to smile again.

NOTHING is more important than being with your family.

It's important to say PLEASE and THANK YOU.

GET TO KNOW people you don't know.

ASK a lot of questions so you can LEARN constantly. There's so much to learn!

Take the time to PRAY.

EVERY DAY is a gift, full of surprises and wonderful new things. Get up early to get a jump on it.

Doing extra little things from the heart; to make OTHERS feel important makes YOU feel great, too.

PLAY and BE SILLY whenever you get the chance. Laughter is contagious.

REST when you are tired so you can give life everything you've got.

SHARE everything—especially your time. It keeps everyone happy, and it's much more fun!

COMMUNICATE constantly so that everyone understands each other.

SING and DANCE at least three times a day and encourage other to join in, even if you have to tug on them a little.

EXPRESS how you feel, no matter what the emotion. It makes it easier for everyone to understand.

BE NICE! There's just no reason to be mean…ever. But if you are, you should get instant punishment to give you time to think, set you straight, and remind you not to do it again.

FLEXIBILITY keeps everybody happy when life's surprises happen. And they will--constantly. Move on to the next great thing!

To get anything, all you need to do is ASK nicely.

Let's remember the basics and take the wonderful examples from the fearless, intelligent, open hearts of any children you come across, and whatever you do, don't try to tell them they're "wrong." That's where WE went terribly wrong in the first place. Never underestimate what you can learn…from anyone. Kids have much to teach us. :) *~Mary Anne*

THE BLAME GAME

Difficult Situations  ***August 2012***

Fill in the blanks with the first things that come to your mind:

I can't _____ because __________________

I don't _______because_________________

He/She won't let me ____________________

I'll never ______ because_________________

Let's call this, "The Blame Game." We all play it…sometimes, our whole life. We blame people, situations, and all kinds of things for all the things we feel we lack. **You bet, crappy things happen to ALL of us, at some point; yes, ALL of us**. No one gets a free, happy pass through life. The Blame Game gives us the false idea that we're the only one that has something to blame for things that make us unhappy. We seriously think that those things don't happen to other people and that's why things are all good for them, don't we? Let's give that a little more thought. Do we really think anybody gets through with a complete "free ride?"

The truth is, no one does. The truth is, challenges are there to play chicken with us. It says, "Okay, here's the dead-on punch, now show me what you got! Show me who you really are!" Obviously, you have options… **you ALWAYS have options.** You can play the Blame Game, nurse your bruise forever, and shut down a part of your life and never try again. The sad truth is, that bruise was probably healed in a few days, but you choose to point it out to everyone for the rest of your life. That doesn't help you or anyone else; in fact, it does a great deal of harm to all of you.

However, if you choose NOT to play the Blame Game, you quickly realize that there's more to you than the world ever dreamed of, and you stand up and RUN through the challenge and after whatever it is you want. You will probably surprise yourself as you see another side of you, but that's the most incredible and fun part of a challenge**. Until you faced the challenge, you had no idea what you were capable of.** So there you have it. That's why we need to face challenges sometimes.

Challenges come in the form of people too. There are so many of us that need to realize we can never win the Blame Game, but there are a lot of really good players out there. The seasoned players have lost all hope of everything. And as they continue making choices that drain them, they automatically have a draining effect on everything and everyone around them. The cold, hard truth is, EVERYTHING we think, do, or say either nourishes us and our lives, or it drains us and our lives. Whatever effect we have on ourselves spills over onto everyone around us, in some shape or form. These people we can politely refer to, as "challenging." You know what I'm talking about. They are a challenge for us, too.

Still, most of the time, we feel like we have to blame SOMETHING. We lash out at God, asking, "What kind of God would create and allow the sad and cruel parts of the world we live in?" We need to STOP for a moment and remember this: God doesn't create those things, PEOPLE create those things. Look at it this way. A loving parent teaches a child everything they know to be happy in life. The parent gives them all the tools they need to make the best life possible, and would die giving this child everything they think will help the child. The child, then, gets to decide how they will live their life and what they will choose, at every moment of their life. GOOD or BAD, the child is the only one that can control the child; the parent cannot fully control what they think or what they do, in any way. Even when the parent's heart is breaking as they watch the child bring harm to their happiness and to others, there is little they can do. But despite those "wrong choices," the parent's love continues simply because they are connected, forever.

God is the ultimate loving parent and we are forever connected to Him as His children; no matter what we or others do. He provides everything we need to be blissfully happy and to live in a state of heaven. We choose daily to accept His gifts or to turn them away. Regardless of the situation, there is ALWAYS A GIFT, somewhere, and sometimes it's the gift of learning through pain because we've turned away from learning through the countless blessings we all have in our lives. This is the harder way to live, but as always, this is our choice. It's much easier to learn through gratitude.

So is it fitting to blame ourselves if we can't define our life as heaven? Yes and No. Yes, we make the choices that bring or push away our happiness, on a daily basis. RISE ABOVE THE SH**! Down-to-earth thinking from Wisconsin touches on the most common things and provides ideas to quickly overcome the simple things that are keeping us from our happiness. We have the choice to use or ignore the tools we have available, including our thoughts.

So I ask you to consider our thoughts as the only thing to blame. Look deep into yourself for a brief minute and realize that everything you think, do, or say is chosen by one of two emotions: **LOVE or FEAR. Thoughts and actions driven by FEAR is the ONLY thing to blame!** The article, **"LOVE YOU,"** explains this more, but the very core of this goes back to our understanding of who we really are. Every single one of us is a blessed and worthy child of God. Nothing we can do can ever remove that birthright. Nothing we can do can ever change who we really are and the potential we have to love and to be loved! If we just take the time every day to remember this, we will automatically make the choices that lead with love, which creates peace for ourselves and for all of the siblings of the world!

That is truly the reason for our life here . . . solely to remember our worth and to evolve into our true and blissful selves, which automatically brings peace to everyone around us, at an infinite level. Our thoughts and our choices DO affect the entire world, at every moment, good or bad. We are always impacting the world! **If you think you do not, it's only because you have forgotten who you are and why you are here.** We truly can't blame anything or anyone for our future, except on things done out of fear. Fear suppresses who we really are, and in turn, harms the world. We have to remember that we ARE human, and thus, we will be learning our entire life. Take the time each day to learn how to choose with love. Our loving Father gives us the tools and the teachings, especially through others, and knows our full potential. He loves us patiently, forever, in hopes that we allow ourselves to love ourselves and to live in the heaven that He designed for us.

So let's all send the Blame Game down the drain for good and instead, look a little more at all of the endless options for today and tomorrow. Sending LOVE to you, because it's the truly the ONLY way to truly LIVE!
~Mary Anne

RELATIONSHIPS!

Relationships 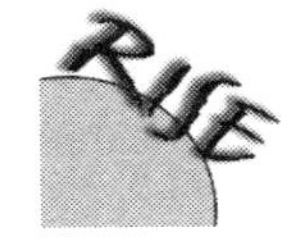 ***October 2012***

So let's talk about relationships for a minute, should we? I mean, we're all experts by now, aren't we? While we're at it, let's cover the whole gamut…not just romantic relationships, but relationships with EVERYBODY! Friends, family, acquaintances, and strangers—let's throw them all in there. Okay, now what? ;)

Well, we know that communication is the key, right? Hmm. Maybe it's the KIND of communication, though. I mean, sarcasm and hidden meanings and digs only make things worse, right? Oh, but it comes so easy when you're hurt or unsure of things! It's so much "easier" to protect yourself and act tough than to be vulnerable. Unfortunately, we hurt ourselves the most when we do this…

I find myself less patient with any kind of discomfort, but especially with discomfort that involves other people. **I realize it's such a waste of everyone's life, not getting along, or even worse, holding back how you really feel, when it's good feelings**. Oh, I annoy the crap out of people close to me sometimes, because they are not always wanting to expose their deepest feelings, but somehow, I drag them through it a little and they love me enough not to ditch me. See, that's the wonder…no matter what, certain people will always love you, just because you're you. I hope you all get this, by now, because it's the very core of harmony with others and peace for you. In reality, people are most comfortable and love you most when you are your true and unique self. So while you find fulfillment in being true to yourself, you help others find peace and inspiration, as well. It's pretty darn cool!

If you've read much of my stuff, you should realize how critical you are to the world. Ya, YOU! It DOES matter if you're doing what makes you genuinely happy. Your happiness has a direct effect on everyone around you, and on the world. This is no exaggeration. If you just think through all the people you affect in one day, you know you can't argue with me. **At every moment, you are either helping or harming yourself or others.** You are either working towards or away from inner peace and happiness, and affecting others in the same way, automatically. I tell ya, there's a reason we are not alone on our own little planet. There's a reason there's so many of us interacting with each other!

So, relationships are really pretty simple; we just make them difficult sometimes. To have the best relationships possible—with anybody—you simply need to be true and genuine to yourself. Does that mean that if someone punches you, you stand up for yourself and punch them back? Well, not quite. You see, in the end, if you hurt that person, you're really not going to feel very good about it, in the end. You'll feel like a schmuck. Deep down inside, you will. So that's not really doing what's best for you.

The way we treat others puts our level of self-respect on display. Catch that? Whenever we do or say anything (and sometimes when we do nothing), everyone can see how much self-love and self-respect we have. Right? Think about things others have done where you were impressed. You know you drew a conclusion that the person is happy, confident, and genuine, didn't you? Now think about the other extreme, when you were appalled by someone's horrible behavior. You came to a very different conclusion that the person is miserable and has some big issues, didn't you?

The truth will always come out, so why not go straight to the source and work on it? Work on you. I try my best to do just a little something, every day, to learn (especially from interaction with others) and to be aware of anything that I'm either not proud of, or that isn't working in one of my relationships. **I don't give the weakness the attention; rather, I ask myself what it could be trying to teach me.** Maybe I haven't shown appreciation to God and/or to the other person. Maybe I'm putting myself down and need to clear my perspective. Maybe I'm not being open-minded enough. Maybe I didn't do or say what my heart was really telling me to do, and I'm worried I won't get the chance now. Maybe I didn't take the time to be grateful and ask God for specifics of what I wanted.

Whatever it is, I have to remember that we are human, we will never be perfect, but because God loves us beyond comprehension, we need to remember to love and accept ourselves and remember that He put each of us here for a very big purpose. When I don't love myself enough to allow my happiness and naturally let "my purpose" occur, I push peace away from me. This pushes peace away from the others around me, at the same time. There's just no getting around it. But the beauty of this perfect design is, when you move towards peace in your life, you automatically move others towards peace as well, ESPECIALLY THOSE YOU HAVE RELATIONSHIPS WITH! It's all pretty darn cool, don't you think?

So my whole search for peace in my life is what created the words for RISE ABOVE THE SH**! Down-to-earth thinking from Wisconsin, and honestly, I wrote it down so I could refer to if, when I need reminders. I still pick it up and re-read it, every now and then. It always helps me understand myself more and to understand what others may be going through, as well.

But if you're looking for a couple of quick ideas today on how to be a little gentler in your relationships, I'll throw a couple of ideas your way:

1. Realize that your loved ones often let you see things you didn't know about yourself…they're kind of like a mirror, sometimes. The things you really love about them, as well as the things that aggravate you,

are probably due to you having that quality, and either loving it or hating it, about yourself.

2. The same principle can be applied to others that you really admire, or really can't stand. It's something within yourself that you recognize, or even an insecurity you have about yourself, that's trying to teach you something more about yourself. Learn the lesson and you're golden.

Regardless of what others do, are we REALLY happy with ourselves when we're rude and disrespectful to others? I don't care how much we think "they deserve it," it still makes us feel icky. Go back to the respect and kindness we usually give to children. MOST of us wouldn't yell or turn our backs on a young child that just didn't know any better. We would gently explain the expectation and suggest what might be better, next time. We might even bring in our feelings, to help them understand how it made you feel. We consider what is best for them, and try our best not to enable bad behavior.

Why do we stop doing this with teens and adults? In my mind, stress, insecurities, bad memories, and the burdens of the world put most of us into a protective state where "we just don't know any better," and thus, we all behave badly sometimes. STOP and remember this, no matter who you're dealing with, and apply the gentleness you would show a child. No matter how they respond, your self-respect will show and you will definitely feel good about your actions. In the end, they will respect you and possibly even learn from you, whether you see the impact directly, or not. Peace to you and your loved ones! ~*Mary Anne*

HELP FOR THE APOCALYPSE

Change 

October 2012

Darkness is just a place where no one is currently shining light, right? Any little bit of light banishes the darkness, immediately and completely. That's the power of love, and it truly does conquer all. When we judge ourselves and when we judge others, we are choosing to remove the light and to create darkness. With darkness, it's difficult for any of us to see things clearly, don't you agree?

The phrase, "The Human Race" defines a GROUP—a CONNECTION. Every human being is connected to every other human being. Think of it as a massive FAMILY UNIT. Think of how in most families, there are sibling rivalries, differences of opinions, different personalities, and just different ways of living and of doing things. (We may not even share the same political and religious views as our parents or brothers or sisters!) EVEN SO, deep down, we still LOVE the members of our family, no matter what, probably because we KNOW there is a BOND forever holding us together.

Here's another way to look at things. We are all God's creatures. He created us with a soul, and through it, we are eternally connected to Him and to every other soul there is. That soul shines a white light inside of all of us, whether we choose to acknowledge it or not, and regardless of how much we each allow it to shine, make no mistake, it is there, in EACH AND EVERY person. That light—that soul—is pure love, so in essence, love is all there truly is, and it's what makes us all ONE. Everything else is an illusion of our perception, <u>usually created when there's not enough light shining on the truth.</u> At the core of it all, we are all one with God, and one with each other.

Therefore, when love is allowed—when the light inside of us is shining or seen—it automatically benefits everyone. Likewise, when love is denied—when the light inside of us is hidden or overlooked—it automatically HARMS everyone. Again, with the mindset that we are ALL one, this includes us, in the benefit AND in the harm.

It's only fitting that ZOMBIES are the focus of The Apocalypse. We are Zombies, some days! Zombies have..."NO SOUL," "LACK THE ABILITY TO THINK FOR THEMSELVES," are. . . "EVIL," and "RESIDE IN DARK PLACES." Sound familiar?

If we can keep this in mind, with everyone we interact with, we look for the love and the truth before judging and harming everyone. We realize that everything negative that appears to be there, is only because no one is shining the light. It doesn't matter whose light it is...any light will make things more clear, and allow more love to reside. The easiest way to do this, is to allow our own light to shine as brightly as possible. We do this by allowing our true selves out, and that automatically happens when we follow the love in our hearts and think, do, and say what we feel warming our hearts. Our true selves realize we are unique, and we know that uniqueness is critical to everyone else in the world. Unforgiveness of others and ourselves (intertwined with fear) causes us to HIDE our true selves…to HIDE our light…to HIDE LOVE. Our unwillingness to forgive can only exist when we ignore that little light that is truly present in every single soul…including ours.

Love yourself instantly by committing to allowing your light to grow. There is no limit to your light, and thus, no limit to love. As you allow your light to shine more brightly, it helps others see things more clearly too, and encourages them to allow their light to shine. Peace and fulfillment are inevitable. Envision the white, bright light growing so much that it consumes your whole body, and casts a bright ray on any shadows you come across. Can you feel everyone's joy and peace?

Think of the purest example of this light . . . a newborn baby. Even as the baby sleeps, he brings love and peace to anyone that gazes upon them. The baby has not been affected by the world yet, and <u>does nothing to hide his light</u>. He is radiant, even while asleep with no movement. We need to remember that this pure, loving being exists in each and every one of us, and with no less power than that of the newborn. It's only our hiding it that allows the darkness, where none of us can see clearly. Fear and lack of forgiveness create an illusion and a darkness that covers our light and the lights of others…especially when something irritates us about others. Truly, what is irritating us is something about ourselves, or our lack of love for ourselves. It creates the darkest of the shadows and hides the truth from others, as well. We HAVE a choice to see our light …we truly are NOT zombies, if we allow ourselves to think and see!

So why not GROW our lights back to their real brightness level? Any negativity of the past cannot affect our present, unless we choose to NOT shine light, love, and the truth. One simple beam instantly dissolves the darkness and allows us to see clearly. RISE ABOVE THE SH**! Down-to-earth thinking from Wisconsin provides TONS of quick ways to do this, through understanding others and ourselves more.

My interpretation of this "apocalypse" is that for those that CHOOSE TO SEE, it is the end of the Dark Era, which has nothing to do with the physical world or our physical bodies. It has to do with remembering there is a soul with light in everyone, and through it, they are forever connected to us. I look forward to more and more people accepting that God is the only source of true peace. We will realize there is more light, love, and awareness of truth than we could ever imagine, right here, inside of us, from our connection to God. More and more are choosing to shine their light, which illuminates the truth for all of us. The truth is, we can be as peaceful and as love-giving as a newborn baby…even more so, as we choose to grow the light beyond comprehension.

Unforgiveness causes us to create "enemies" and to try to punish others, but in reality, we punish ourselves the most. We hide the light when we don't forgive, and through it, punish ourselves with toxins, stress, and self-destructive behavior and negative relationships. Maybe we think if we punish ourselves, we can lessen our guilt? The guilt is only there because we are not acknowledging our light and the present moment. The present moment tells us that no matter what we or anyone DID in the PAST, it does not affect our current status and our current choices, unless we decide to punish ourselves more, unnecessarily…does that make any sense at all? Forgiving doesn't mean that you're taking the blame or accepting what happened…it simply means you value yourself and your life enough to leave it behind and not let it punish you now. The blame can go to one source: Light was not shining where it could have been. The reason is irrelevant. It's over and done. Let it be over and done! Come out of the "Dark Era!"

Think of the intense GLOW of the realness we could create, all shining our lights, together. I am excited for "The Apocalypse!" I have hope for the survival of souls of my family…the whole human race. *~Mary Anne*

WHERE ARE YOU?

Awareness  ***January 2013***

Where are you? Who are you pretending to be? Why are you hiding? How long do you plan to live this way, and deprive the world (and especially those immediately around you) of the REAL you? : (Isn't it time to find the REAL YOU? Hasn't life been hard enough, already? REAL is easy. REAL is fun. REAL is peaceful. REAL is fulfilling. Trust me for just a moment or two, and read on, please. I know for a fact that we need the REAL YOU…every bit of you.

When we allow ourselves to be our REAL person, life is incredible. You wake up happy and excited for the day, even if it is a work day. You learn to forgive yourself of anything you may have said or done before this moment in time, because you know it doesn't matter anymore. You don't worry about anything ahead of this moment in time, because you are assured that as long as you TRY to be your true self, everything will be just fine. It doesn't bother you what other people say or do to you, since you know that anything negative they do is really an issue they have with themselves; it's not really about you. You think I'm dreaming or out of touch with reality? It's so ironic, because just the opposite is true; anyone that is hiding from their true self and their real life is truly not awake and not really present in this real life.

It took me years to wake up—40-something years, sadly, but I don't beat myself up for that. There's no point, since something I did even yesterday doesn't have anything to do with today. Today, I have full control (as I always do) to be and do whatever I want; we all do, we just don't always realize it. Instead, we follow what the rest of the world is saying or doing. We seriously ignore our heart, our soul, and think we need to do and be whatever the majority thinks. Tell me, what would you rather be? "Right" according to the miserable world that couldn't possibly know who you really are, or "Right" according to your heart, which brings you peace? Why ignore your heart—the only holder of your truth?

We think that if we get cancer, we need to listen to the medical statistics and accept dying before we really want to. We think we have to spend the majority of our day doing things we don't want to do, with people we don't want to be with, with tons of stress and worry in our lives. We think we have to be that mean-and-in-control parent or boss or customer. We think we have to put all of our dreams and desires on hold until "later in life." We think we can't find God or anything good, the majority of the time. Sound familiar? HOW LONG DO YOU PLAN TO LIVE THIS WAY?

And WHY are you living this way? Maybe you're just a little lost, like I was--lost in the thinking of the world? Maybe you stomped out the truth of your heart because the rest of the world didn't agree, like I used to? Are you happy? Are you really, really happy? If not, I challenge you to WAKE UP! Come back to reality—I mean REALity, not using the negative definition the world has given to the word, referring to pain and suffering and disappointment! Doesn't it just make your stomach turn, that REALITY is accepted as a reference to something bad? It's so backwards and so untrue! I know, because I am truly living in the REAL WORLD, which is miraculous and joyful, every day I choose this…really, it is!

So first off, please stop punishing yourself, thinking you deserve the crappy life the world likes to create. I don't care what you've ever done, BE DONE WITH IT! It really is as easy as just deciding you are done suffering and you are done making others suffer. Every single moment, you choose one way or the other: You choose to make life miserable or miraculous. Tell yourself, "I choose to make life miraculous!" I mean, WHY NOT? What have you got to lose? You can't lose yourself any more than you already have, can you? If you feel you owe people something to make up for what you've done, well then do it, if it makes you feel better. If they're no longer around, then help someone else. Do whatever you need to, to feel like you've earned the right to stop punishing yourself. You know, I'm going to talk about God here for a second, because nearly all of us do believe in Him. I do, so I really don't care if this article offends that one person in a million that doesn't want to hear God's name—I choose to be my REAL self, and any respectful person would not be offended by that.

God tells us over and over again, "I forgive you, no matter what you've done." God loves us, UNCONDITIONALLY, as His beautiful children. He created each and every one of us to live this life for two reasons: To help us on our journey to find our REAL and TRUE SELVES and to HELP THE WORLD. All you need to accomplish both is to let the love of your heart OUT. First and foremost, you have to direct that love at yourself, remember you are human, and FORGIVE YOURSELF! If God forgives you for everything, you need to follow His example and forgive yourself too, however you need to do it! STOP HIDING! STOP WASTING YOUR LIFE! Don't die with regrets; don't choose to live with misery! Say this now, "I choose to live with miracles!" God is always right next to you…well actually, He's WITHIN you; He is part of you. But there's not a darn thing He can do when you choose to stumble through life without Him. His mind-blowing gift of free will requires that you ASK HIM to be part of your day, and part of your life. In order to ask Him for something, you need to be very clear on what it is you want, and why, and then, "Ask and Ye shall receive."

This ask-and-receive thing is in place ALL THE TIME, not just when you ask for good or happy things. Be warned, that if your brain is always full of worry, stress, sad or bad thoughts, lack of desire to get up and live a new day, focus on illness, lack, or feeling like you don't deserve things, guess what you'll get? You will get whatever you think about. Free will gives you the life you ASK for. Please choose your thoughts wisely; ask

God to guide you and help you stay on top of them! I can't do it without Him, and I do have miracles in my life, every day I do this. For me, it's the only way to live!

So back to finding the REAL YOU. Oh, I hope you give it a try. . . I know for a fact, the world absolutely needs you to do something big in this life, or you wouldn't be here, so please do yourself the favor of forgetting everything the world ever told you, and start asking your heart for its opinion. It'll never steer you wrong, and it will always take good care of you. There's more on all this in a short video I shot, on a new website I'm working on for Teens. Click on the link called, "You Are Here For a Reason" in the upper-right-hand corner of this page: http://teensriseabove.com/. Even though I'm addressing Teens, it applies to everyone, and if nothing else, I'd love your opinions—any opinions.

My first book, RISE ABOVE THE SH**! Down-to-earth thinking from Wisconsin, also gives tons of ideas to overcome any SH** that's been keeping you from being your true self, and there'll be lots more in the book I'm currently working on. I learn more every single day, on how to listen to my heart and soul, and it brings me nothing but absolute peace and all the great things that come with it. Just when I think life can't be any more miraculous, something even better happens, and I remember that I'm just getting started with all this life has to offer, when we strive to be our real selves. God has put us in paradise; only we create the hell some of us live in. Choose miracles, not misery. The world is waiting, and the world absolutely, positively NEEDS THE REAL YOU. Please take advantage of everything I've learned so far with all the free reading you want. My book is available at a lot of libraries, and I'll gladly donate one to those that don't have it. There are lots of free notes like this on my website, AnniePress.com, and lastly, you can friend me on Facebook through the AnniePress.com site, and message me with your comments and questions. It all helps me, so I appreciate all feedback and inspiration! So glad you're here, and I'm thrilled for the life you will start living now!

With love ~Mary Anne

YOU ARE WHAT YOU . . .

Awareness

January 2013

We've all heard the saying, "You are what you eat!" This note is <u>not</u> about eating; it's more about who you are, how you got that way, and how you CHOOSE to stay that way. It's so darn simple, you probably won't believe it, until you try it out, honestly.

If you've read my book, RISE ABOVE THE SH**! Down-to-earth thinking from Wisconsin, you have read my advice about free will. Free will isn't something you can turn on and off; it is constantly working, whether you choose to acknowledge it, or not. Now there's a little more to it, but as a quick refresher, your life, and your very self, becomes whatever you focus on the most. You end up wherever your deepest desires and beliefs go. Good or bad, happy or sad, whatever main topics you think about the most becomes your life. Sound too easy? Be honest with yourself, and look at where you are in life. Think of what goes the way you want, and the things that don't. Now, the hard part. Dig DEEP into you past thoughts and beliefs and worries and dreams. The ones with the most attention had the most power, and they created the life you have, or have lived. DIG DEEP. This exercise is not to make you feel bad, it's simply to allow you to open up to the possibility, so that you can change things to the way you want, NOW! Now is all that matters!

Some say, "God is in control." I do believe, He certainly is. But here's the thing: He has given us the gift of free will. He has told us that WE get to decide. This is how much He loves us; He never forces anything on us…not ever. He has given us the responsibility for our own lives. "Ask and Ye Shall Receive." He loves us so much, He lets us decide if we want good or bad, happy or sad. EACH person CHOOSES for themselves, their whole life.

So, it's only common sense that tells us, then, that we are what we:

EAT and DRINK: The body needs good fuel to produce good cells, and to ward off any germs or disease or toxins; anything of less quality starves the cells, and makes them unable to fight off harmful things, and we get sick. Putting harmful things in the body, like most drugs, alcohol, processed foods and drinks, etc. WILL HARM YOUR BODY, sooner or later. What other choice does it have? Most people cause their own death, just through the choices of what they eat and drink. Very sad, but very true. As long as you are alive, your cells are growing, fighting, and regenerating. What are you giving them to work with?

BELIEVE: If we think we need to suffer or be punished, or that God isn't present in our lives, it is exactly what we will get. If you want an idea on a new belief, I'll throw my thinking your way. First of all,

God never said we should suffer; He said we are precious, and it's critical to the world that we are happy. He said we need to love ourselves and our neighbors. He said, no matter what you've done, I forgive you, and thus, we need to forgive ourselves (and others!) Second, God is always here, everywhere, but if we push Him away and tell Him we don't need His help, He can't provide it. He is within every single one of us, so where do you think He's gonna go?

WATCH: Screen time is killing our society, in so many ways! Not only does the electronic junk distract, drain, and scramble our brains, but it's overpowering our free will. What you focus on, you will get. It doesn't make any difference if it's real or not; you are still choosing to focus on it, therefore, you are asking for it! Watching dramas and people making fun of, or being mean to other people, watching violence and sad stories…again, whether it's real or in a movie, it doesn't matter! You are taking your precious brain and feeding it hours and hours of something that WILL NOT HELP YOU OR YOUR LIFE, at the same time you are depriving yourself of the time you could be spending doing something that WILL help your life. It's bad and even worse! Why are you trying to drown out your brain, anyway? Many world experts are blaming the violence we allow our kids to experience through TV, movies, internet, video games on what helps them think it's okay to grab a gun and kill whoever's bothering them. What else do you have to blame for this epidemic of gun slaughters that has become a norm in U.S. Society? Is it such a far stretch to think that the satisfaction they see in a violent movie after the hero's killed a bunch of bad guys might give them a little nudge when they're in unbearable emotional pain?

READ or LISTEN TO: Radio, books, and conversations are also almost always positive or negative. Truly, if you keep listening to sad or angry songs on the radio, those same things will show up in your life, over and over again. If you read sad and bad news, listen to chronic complainers and angry or mean people, including those that love to judge others and gossip, you will have more and more of that in your life, and you'll find yourself becoming those people. You always have the choice to turn the radio station or put in and inspirational book on CD. You always have the choice in who you hang around and have conversations with. Even if the downer person must remain in your life, you don't have to copy their bad behavior. You even have the right to inform them you don't want to talk about other people and you can change the subject or even give them a copy of this note! :)

I think you get the idea, but just to drive it home, let me ask you this: If you were responsible for a 3-year old that you really loved, and wanted everything good for the child, would you feed them all the things you eat and drink? Let them watch the violent or dramatic shows you watch? Listen to all the conversations you have? Tell them God wants them to suffer in this life? Well, would you? I'm sure you'll say no, and perhaps you'll even say that you know better than a 3-year old, so it's different? I hate to tell you, but it is the soul that we're feeding with our choices, and even if our human brain can tell us when something's real or not, our soul is still receiving EVERYTHING we focus on. Our soul is no different than a 3-year old's, other than we've fed it a lot more crap in our human years. No matter the age, the soul knows everything it's been exposed to, especially love. If we don't show our own soul a little love, it will think it is unworthy and that a sad life is what it's meant to live. Happy or sad, real or not, the soul is exposed. Your life will go to what your soul feels. It's free will; it's always your choice. Like it or not, you are responsible for your own soul and your own life. Your soul yearns for your dreams and for your happiness in this life; what have you got to lose in giving it what it wants now? Yes, Virginia, no matter how long you've ignored it, you do have a soul; the very same soul with the very same dreams, and the very same love that you had as a 3-year old.

So what do you do? It's very simple; just start making choices that will bring you the happy life you want. Big or small, any change for the better kicks butt! Just take the time, throughout the day to ask yourself, "Is this helping my life, in any way?" If you can't answer yes, think about what other options you have, and then, DO IT! Shut off the TV. Quit reading the newspaper and hanging out with negative people. Get rid of the video games. Go to happy, inspiring movies. Learn something through a book, workshop, the internet, or a person you know. Exercise. Start buying better food and don't restock anything toxic in your house. Shut OFF the electronics, get a good night's sleep, and get outside and REALLY look around at nature, every day. Think only about what you WANT because those things make you happy and take you to the life of your dreams. Make no mistake. Every moment, you are either feeding your soul or draining it. Your soul has been waiting long enough! Now, do only what helps you and your life and start living! *~Mary Anne*

HELPING (AND PUTTING UP WITH) LOVED ONES THAT HURT YOU

Relationships 

March 2013

Please tell me, God, what to do with some people, sometimes? **You never give us more than we can handle, but You sure know how to push us right to the edge, where we think we can't handle it, don't You?** Please God, I don't want people to judge me. I just want them to love me for who I am and for the goodness that always exists, deep down within me, so please, remind me not to judge and to just love people for who they are, and for the goodness that always exists, deep down within everyone!

As I'm writing this to share with others, I already know I'm going to tick somebody off again. I try to respect people's time and get to the point quickly, but not everybody likes that, and are offended that I seem to be scolding them. I try to offer a viewpoint that helps me realize something new about people and myself, but not everybody wants my viewpoint, and some take it personally. I feel compelled to offer thoughts that may spark ideas to overcome our own worst enemy (our own self), in an effort to help people find peace and happiness, but not everybody wants that, and it only upsets them. I try my best to respect everyone's right to live the life they choose, but knowing that someone helped me a great deal with feedback (good or bad), sometimes I can't keep my mouth shut when someone complains or is unhappy. **One thing I feel strongly about is that we are here to help each other, and I feel worse not trying to help, even when my thoughts are not welcome; but to my disappointment, not everybody wants help.**

Not everybody wants to help others or to be helped. Not everybody wants other viewpoints or change in their life. Not everybody is comfortable being around happy, peaceful people. ***Not everybody wants happy.*** I have to respect that people have the right to choose, to not judge them, and to love them, all the same. Sometimes this is a random stranger that you can walk away from and say a prayer for, to feel better about not sticking your nose into their business; but more often, it's a coworker, a friend, a child, or even a spouse. Then what? How can you respect their right to misery and suffering when they are directly impacting you on a daily basis? How can you stand by, day after day, as they disrespect and mistreat and bring you down, because they are not capable of anything else? After a while, it wears on you. After a while, it drains you and frustrates you to the point that you start acting like someone you truly are not. Sh** rubs off, after a while, but still, we have no one to blame for our attitude or actions; we are always responsible for that. **But wait, how come they can blame everything and everyone, and go on and on**

about who's right and who's wrong, but we have to suck it up and be nice and loving? It's SO unfair, and frankly, it really burns my butt, every now and then. Then we worry, are we being too nice and enabling their bad behavior? Is our lack of expressing how "wrong" and "messed up" they are just making them worse? Please God, tell me what to do with these people! I am still human, and I still have a breaking point, and today, I'd just like to tell a few of them how I feel about it!

But wait. Then I'm the bad guy. Then I'm the problem, and now, I've just given them one more person and bad situation to blame their misery on. Yea, that never works, and to top it all off, I'd only feel worse about everything, then. No, there has to be a better way. Compassion? I try. I keep telling myself that everyone's life and awareness of life is very different from mine, and that they are doing the best they can, under the circumstances of their life and mindset. **But are they really doing the best they can, or are they just slacking off, to put the rest of us through hell?** Misery does love company, after all. There it is again, though: MISERY. I guess I'd rather have people be threatened by my being too happy than risk being miserable, myself. I guess I need to accept that no matter how much we preach that uniqueness is a blessing, someone is always going to be upset, just because someone or something is different. There's no way that any one of us could always please everyone, after all, so it's a waste of life to even try.

Still, we know how to help others to fix things in their life, to find peace, and to be happy. We ALL know something that would help many, many people find this "secret to life," so it's very hard to not want to help. Most of us know that if more people are happy, they would be nicer to others, and in turn, the world could be a much better place for everyone, and thus, people would better understand their invaluable worth to the rest of the world. Even so, not everyone wants a better world. Not everyone wants a happier life. Not everyone wants "better." So, those people will continue to be angry and lash out at others, just as long as they choose. They may even affect others enough to shake their truth about who they are, and bring them over to join them, on the dark side. **Sometimes, it feels that way, like it's you against an impossible dark force, which challenges you to think again about who you are and how you want your life to be.** It tries to lie to you enough, to where you start to break down and start blaming others for your lack of happiness or lack of progress towards your dreams. It presses you against the wall and forces you to "CHOOSE!"

Do you want to join the masses of misery, out of fear, or do you want to prove to yourself that you love yourself and others enough to stand firm in who you want to be? Will you continue to be the true, loving person you want to be, and to do the things that bring you lasting joy and peace, regardless of what may be going on around you? Will you remain responsible for your life? Will you respect yourself and others enough to love and appreciate the lessons you learn, no matter what anyone else thinks or says? I truly believe that if I stick to keeping my heart and perspective open, I can only have a positive effect on my life and others, no matter what goes on, and no matter how unsettling it may be to someone that is struggling and not willing or able to be their true self. **Perhaps they have chosen to suffer in this lifetime, and must make their world a miserable place; perhaps they have chosen to help others learn to stand firm in who they are, by constantly criticizing and challenging the very core of their beliefs.** Perhaps they are doing me a favor and helping me learn, and this is their way to be a martyr in this lifetime. It's unlikely I will ever know, or ever understand, but that's where faith, compassion, and love come in.

I need to practice loving and not judging, no matter what someone is doing or not doing, and no matter what type of life they have chosen to live. I believe this is what we call, "unconditional love," and I believe it is the true test of our understanding that we are all here to help each other, in whatever which way that may be. Everyone has a soul, after all, and at the very core of that soul is goodness; I cannot doubt that, just because it may be hidden from my small human eyes and my small human mind. Some things are meant to be believed, even when we cannot see them. Following your heart and believing is what leads us to fulfillment and peace, especially when we realize it's not about the outside world or anything going on in it. Truly, it's all about what we have within us, and I suppose that people like me would never realize this, if everyone was nice to me all the time. **I would be misled into thinking that all my happiness was coming from other people, and worse, that I had to rely on them for where my life went.** I would be miserable, frustrated, and depressed, waiting for someone to fix my life and tell me who I was, and to let me be who I really am. But it would never happen, because no one can ever do this for you, and I wouldn't know it. That would be the worst. I would give up all hope, I think. I might even be angry at happy people, because it would feel so unfair that someone or something made their life great and now, mine couldn't be, because it was all used up on them. Life would suck!

I remind myself, that every interaction and every experience with others must be a mutually beneficial interaction, so it must be assisting me, somehow? I also remind myself that fear only comes out when someone doesn't feel safe; some people do not feel safe having to look at their feelings. Are they blind? Can't they see what they are doing and how much they are hurting others? Are they deaf? Why doesn't anything we say to help them and to help the situation seem to be heard? Are they dumb (mute)? Why can't they let the true feelings of their heart, the ones they swear they feel for you, be spoken out loud? Are they paralyzed? At least if they can't make words come out of their mouth, couldn't they make the smallest gesture towards showing a little kindness?

I can find compassion for someone that truly doesn't realize what they are doing because they really are unaware of what they are doing by envisioning them as emotionally blind, deaf, dumb, and paralyzed, that is, until, they go the other way. Hiding feelings so far down that you can't find them or use them is one thing. **Actions that seem to want to see others hurt, or take what you ask for and use it against you, or say hurtful, mean things, or make gestures or situations that they know will offend you, is another.** Now they seem to be fighting you, like an enemy that needs to be conquered, sending you feelings that cannot be received as anything other than hate.

This is when my humanness loses all hope for being able to hold on to who I am while I am still with this person. **This is the biggest obstacle in staying true to who I am, that I can think of: When someone you love, that has said they love you displays the opposite, a lot of the time.** My heart goes into hiding, just to survive, and covering it up automatically drains and depresses me. I know it's not right, and I know I cannot stay there too long; life is too valuable and too short, and I do know that I don't want to waste it. I have to do something to respect and love myself. I have to do something to respect and love the handicapped person that may be too far gone. Allowing things to go on and on, doing nothing but simply praying for change, only hurts the both of you, along with everyone else in your environment. No matter what, we always have an effect on others, in some form. **No, when we have the awareness to see, hear, say, and do, we need to do whatever we can, regardless of the pain we may be**

feeling. Other people really do rely on someone to do something.

I have to remind myself that darkness is nothing more than a place where someone is not shining light. Sometimes to survive the hurt we are feeling, we have to hide our light until we feel strong enough again to let the world know we are there. I know I have to do it sometimes, but even then, I have to remind myself that it is temporary and I refuse to stay there. **Guess what happens if I stay there? I start to slip into a habit of not listening to my heart, and start hiding my true feelings.** I am not truly myself, and therefore, I cannot really live the life I was intended to life. I slowly decide to become blind, deaf, dumb, and paralyzed myself!

Oh my God! Just the thought of existing like that terrifies me! The thought of the misery I'd cause myself physically makes me sick to my head and stomach! NO! NO! Oh my God! It breaks my heart to think that the person I'm struggling with is that unhappy, even some of the time, but doesn't have a clue! How do they get up in the morning? How numb must they be to go through even a day like that? Is that why so many lose themselves in their electronics, addictions, depression, sickness, and isolation . . . just to get through another miserable day? It's heart-wrenching! **They don't know how to change, even if they realize it can be changed. They are paralyzed, after all.**

It's easy to recognize them. They are the ones that complain about everything, but never consider a solution. They are the ones constantly finding fault with everyone, and everything, and pointing it out to anyone that will listen. They are the ones that complain that there's "nothing to do," but are always too busy to have time to spend with you or on things they should be doing. Instead, they try to busy themselves with whatever will keep their mind off of thinking too much; quiet time alone or with someone that may try to get them thinking must be avoided, at all costs. Oh my God! Yes, they push us to our max!

Now that my anger and disappointment has been strongly defeated with this reasoning, I can see a little more clearly again. My sight is slowly returning, and so is my compassion. I remember that any damage that an unaware person does is the worst to themselves. What I'm feeling is nothing, compared to what they are, or eventually will feel. **Truly, some go to their grave, never allowing their light to shine because of this.**

That's where we desperately need each other. When someone doesn't realize they even have a light, we need to shine ours bright enough for them to hopefully use a little of it to see, hear, speak, and move. Huddled in their darkness, they have forgotten what it even feels like to do all this. Do we have to be a martyr and live a life of neglect, criticism, hurt, suppression, and hopelessness, turning all of our light onto them? NO, NO, NO! Harming yourself while helping others is never the answer. **You cannot "love another as yourself" if you don't love yourself enough to respect yourself enough to stay in a place where you are able**

to be your true self. First and foremost, you need to listen to your heart and be your real self, or your light goes out, too. It is critical that your heart shine, and shine brightly! How else are you going to provide light to others?

We are only human, so sometimes this is impossible to do with someone you love hurting you. It's up to you to find a way. I know this sounds like an unfair responsibility, but the paralyzed person can't help, usually. **This is where you finally can see a little more of the intense goodness and strength you already have within you.** I've heard it said that negative situations and people are our much-needed and most influential teachers. Based on my personal experiences, I have to say it has been this way in my life, for sure. I prefer to learn and grow, and not drag out the confusing and frustrating phases of my life. I do know that I have firmly learned invaluable things and moved on very quickly to change my life for the better, because of the negative experiences in my life.

Oh, and my secret to not losing it completely when I'm being pushed to my limit…I ask God to be with me, to handle it, and guide me to do what's best for everyone. Most of the time, I'm most comfortable asking the angels, as I'm still working on not feeling like I'm pestering God with little stuff (which is altogether silly), but it's all the same. He can handle anything, any size, any person, and if you ask and expect miracles, you will get them! Keep your light shining in your heart, good and bright—we all need you, so badly!

Need ideas on dealing with people or just following your heart, especially when it's hurting? **There are tons of my thoughts on this in the book, RISE ABOVE THE SH**! Down-to-earth thinking from Wisconsin, and in free articles on our website, AnniePress.com. I also have a very rough video on the top corner of the TeensRiseAbobe.com site, called, "You Are Here For A Reason!"** It teaches how to learn to listen to your heart, versus the lies in your head. Take the time to love yourself enough to reach out for new ideas when life isn't blissful…lack of bliss is your first clue that you are not following your heart!

Be ready, as some may perceive your turn towards self-love as turning away from them. This is what I call, "tough love," because it's tough to outwardly appear as though you're withholding love by not enabling further disrespectful behavior. In reality you're pouring out love for both yourself and the other person, by being strong about what will be best for the two of you (and in reality, for everyone else then). It's enlightening to realize that by not doing anything about the situation, and allowing the less-than-loving treatment from our loved ones, we are asking for more of the same, and so, we are now doing whatever we can, out of love, to change things for the better. But again, sometimes this is very unsettling to our loved ones, as their fear of change itself tips their world on its edge. Sometimes, their terror of having to think about how they feel is too much, and they rebel and resent you. **It may hurt for a little while, to watch someone chose misery over**

realizing they are in control of their life, but we have to stay focused on the long-term benefits. Even if they never realize what you have tried to do for them, if will affect the both of you (and again others around you) in a good way, ultimately. Following the heart never fails and draws in more love, and more love will always bring peace. Even if the love is never returned from the person because their emotional handicaps keep them from being anything but angry at you, you will know you did your best, and that's all that matters. That's what brings you peace.

We have to remember that no one, and no one, has our experiences, our awareness, our challenges, our dreams, our successes, our hurts, or our exact way of thinking. We cannot possibly expect others to see exactly what we see, regardless of how obvious we believe it is. Everyone is on their own path; everyone has their own free will. **Everyone must live the way they choose, no matter what we think about it.** Our role, as someone that crosses their path, is to stay true to our heart so that our light shines as brightly as possible. There will be many that need and use that light, whether we realize it or not. **So there it is again, right in my face: All that matters is love and compassion, for ourselves first, because it naturally touches everyone else we come in contact with.** Stay true to yourself. The world is absolutely depending on you.

With love, and I'd really appreciate your feedback on this one! ~Mary Anne

STAY CALM, AND LEAVE A PATH OF LIGHT

Difficult Situations  ***April 2013***

Two of my best friends complimented me recently, saying that I stay calm and am very understanding when others may be behaving badly. Honestly, it surprised me, because I am quite human when it comes to being hurt or wronged. I get angry; I get sad; I do and say things I am not proud of. But I accept the fact that I am human, and that we're all human, and I try to get over it, as quickly as possible. I think it comes from one simple fact of my life: I know that any negative anything is keeping me from the peace and happiness I want in my life. I know that it robs me clean of really living the amazing moments that are intended for me (and for ALL of us), every moment the unloving feelings are allowed in my life. That alone, motivates me to resolve, ignore, brush off, or walk away from whatever stands between me and my real life.

But how do we not want justice, sometimes, if not all the time? How do we stop that anger that human nature sparks to help us defend ourselves? How do we calmly sit by and not want to stop people and "teach them a lesson?" Again, I am human, but I do the best I can. And guess what? All the other humans out there are also doing the best *they* can. Don't buy it? They SHOULD know better. They COULD try harder. They acted out of SPITE. They were WRONG. This isn't

RIGHT. They need to know how it FEELS. I need to TEACH them a LESSON. Someone needs to STOP them. I know you know how it feels to be on the crappy receiving end. I know you've been there, far too many times. But fear not…I have some good news for you!

First, how did I get where I am, in my seemingly-naive state of mind? Well, I worked on it, a long time, again, in a mission to never let anything or anyone else affect my happiness. Truly, they can't; we decide what we allow or don't allow. I piled lots of my thinking into the book, RISE ABOVE THE SH**! Down-to-earth thinking from Wisconsin. We are always the boss of ourselves, and our lives, no matter what. I have to credit Marianne Williamson's book, A Return to Love, and specifically her chapter on "Relationships" as something that really helped me find compassion for wrong-doing, instead of anger or sadness. If you're not familiar with it, she summarizes her take of A Course in Miracles, an in-depth read I hope to get to, some day.

Next, it helps to remember that even when someone does something TO you, it's not ABOUT you. IT'S TRULY ABOUT THEM. Stop and think about it next time; do you see the misery inside the wrong-doer? You will see it, clear as day, if you don't block your vision with a negative feeling. You may also remember, that any negative things harm the attacker much more than the person being attacked. Usually, whatever they're accusing or attacking you with is how they feel about themselves. They are really attacking and exposing themselves, merely using you as a scapegoat. How unhappy do you have to be, to voluntarily hurt yourself? Pretty unhappy…and that's what I'm trying to get at. People are out of their minds with fear, sadness, regrets, resentments, lies, insecurities, and a whole SH** pile of things they're doing to hurt themselves and ruin their lives, and usually, they are so far gone they don't even realize it! They truly are OUT OF THEIR HEART, and thus, OUT OF THEIR MIND!

And so I repeat, "They are doing the best they can, in their current emotional and mental state!" Really, everyone is. Some people's mental and emotional states are just more positive than others. Some are blessed enough to find their way back to their heart, however that may happen, and so, they choose to treat people better, no matter what. Or at least they try. Human imperfections will always play a part, but a good part. If we were all perfect, we'd never learn a thing, would we? What would the point of this life be, if we already knew and understood everything? WHAT IF the whole point of this life is to learn to love yourself completely, and then automatically, everyone else, too? WHAT IF? How are you coming along?

But why do these awful things happen, especially to nice people, like you? Ah, another awesome question that I can't try to provide an answer to. I can tell you how I cope with it, though, personally. I'd like to quote Tami Gulland, a Spiritual Business Coach (www.AngelsForSuccess.com), who said, "Look for the gift. There's always a gift." I find this to be true, in my life, no matter what it is, and so, I try to keep my heart and mind open to what the situation is GIVING me. Is it a lesson I need to learn, about myself or about someone else? Is there something I need to take action on, or pay attention to? Is clarification or communication needed? Will something that happened alter someone's path or provide a stepping stone towards something better? There are endless possibilities, and I'll be honest. When it's something really hard to understand at the moment, I have adopted a quick go-to. I talk to the big guy and say, "God, I don't understand this. Please ease my pain and confusion. I know You know what You're doing, and I trust You always know what's best; help me understand, eventually. Please help me keep my heart open and see the gifts and learn from them."

I could not have gotten through a recent, nasty verbal attack without my heart. At first, I thought they were just expressing the same disappointment I had, with the choices one of their loved ones had made. I soon realized their loved one seemed to have told everyone the exact opposite of the truth. Something--their emotional state or just being too scared to tell everyone what they really want—caused them to run with any twisted excuse, instead of just telling everyone how they really feel, and what really occurred. Sad as the whole thing is, I couldn't fault my attacker for the hate that had built up in their heart; they have been terribly mislead by someone they trust. I was absolutely baffled, as I analyzed the extent of unnecessary harm that had occurred to so many people, out of this post-ponement of the truth of what the dishonest person wants. They have to know, the truth will come out, eventually?

Sure, I tried to lead this person to the truth, but they'd have nothing of it. The verbal conversation was pointless, to the extent that I stopped and asked, "What do you hope to accomplish, with this conversation?" I asked this a couple of times, only to be badgered by an attempt to manipulate me into saying what they wanted to hear…something to justify and feed their anger and bitterness. But I had nothing for this person but the truth, and they quickly turned away from it, even when I tried to explain that they didn't know all the facts, and that what they were saying and believing was not true. One look in their eyes told me there was no point in continuing the conversation. Their own insecurity and misery didn't want help, resolution, or the truth. I paused to breathe and think, and heard a clear message, "Just stop talking." I did, and that was the end of it.

It is incomprehensible to me that one person can choose a path that hurts so many people, and then blame it on someone else and portray themselves as the victim, but I have to believe there is a reason for all of it. Sure, I was sad. Sure, I was enraged. But only briefly. In my heart, I choose to leave a path of light, not a path of SH** behind, as often as humanly possible. Already, I can see the many gifts that have come out of this icky situation, so all is well, and all will be well.

I chose, right then and there, not to accept the SH** that was being flung at me. I can't tell you how awesome that feels…it is an outward expression of self-respect and love. You are going to have to just try it out yourself to see! I have come to learn that as humans, we will often cling to the familiar, no matter how bad it is, rather than take the courage to try to change something for the better. We sometimes choose to wallow in our misery, playing the victim, as if someone or something else is to blame for our unhappiness. I plead with all of you…that's just not how it is. Only we have control of our own hearts, and thus, our own lives. If I can share this insight with just one person today, the world instantly changes for the better, as one more person realizes how amazing this life really is, when we simply allow it. In the meantime, send LOVE to all those that wrong you; while we all need love, I feel like they could use a little extra. *~Mary Anne*

WANT TO CANCEL-OUT CANCER? DITCH DISEASE? WASH OFF WEIGHT?

Health ***May 2013***

I've had a lot of health stuff brought to my attention in recent months; so much so that I'm kind of wondering if I'll end up writing a whole book on it? I figured I'd start with this article and see what happens, so here goes.

Health is such a simple thing, in my mind. The ways of the world have just messed it up so bad, that most people don't know which way is up anymore. It's not just all the poisonous products, food and drink, and medicines. It's the whole thought process behind how to "fix" something. It seems that we try to treat a particular health issue as though it has nothing at all to do with the rest of the body, and that the body isn't affected by anything else. It's absurd to me, because obviously, it is connected to the rest of the body, and the body is in an environment at all times. So how do I hit on everything in one article? You know it's hard for me to be brief! But I'm going to try! Let's just make a list of some of the basics:

1. **The Junk in our Food and Drinks:** God put food on the earth for us in a form that nourishes the body, giving it all it needs to repair itself from just about anything. The fresher (and more organic!) and raw and simple the food, the finer the nourishment. The more tiny cells of the food you break open as you eat it, the more nutrients you release; that's why chewing things slowly and very fine or even juicing are so beneficial. When we process and add junk (mostly unnatural and therefore, poison to our bodies) we not only cook all the nutrients out, but we add things our body doesn't recognize, and so it's identified as a toxin. Most people eat and drink nothing but toxins, all day long. (Soda and most packaged drinks are a great example.)

2. **Overload of Toxins in Eating:** Yes, the body has very complex systems to remove all these toxins, but Holy Smokes! Most of us take in way more than the body can handle. Our choices of food and drink alone make it nearly impossible for it to keep up, but we also go without "oiling" that system by not giving it enough plain water, good fats, oxygen, nutrients, and FRESH, NATURAL antioxidants through the raw food we should be eating. On top of that, did you know the body can only detox when it's not digesting? So if you don't go long enough between eating, your body probably doesn't ever finish detoxing. How do you know how you're doing? Swelling, bloating, allergies, inflammation of any kind, feeling yucky or unenergetic, and illness of any kind are some great big warning signs that should never be ignored. A body that is nourished and cared for

properly can detox, fight off, and heal anything, including cancer.

3. **Other Big Sources of Toxins:** Anything else we eat, drink, inhale, and absorb through our skin gets in our body. This includes medicine and supplements, chemicals in the air and in soap, makeup, lotion, cleaners, household products, and anything else. Just because it's prescribed or for sale it doesn't mean it's safe! No one is monitoring what your body is getting slammed with and giving you any kind of warning about the deathly impact it could have on you! This is where you need to be responsible for yourself and your family!

4. **Give Yourself Plenty of the Good Stuff:** There are foods out there that are listed as "Super Foods" and "Good Fats" and "Antioxidants." I know I've done enough damage over the years to need a lot of these things now, and again, the best way is through the organic, raw, as fresh and as-alive-as-possible foods! I read that flax seed, fresh-ground only, can shrink and even KILL cancer cells. Since I bought a cheap coffee grinder and started sprinkling a teaspoon a day on my food, I have noticed less swelling in my lymph nodes, so it must be doing something! I also want to try out ginger, turmeric, and aloe vera, since I read they are miracle foods. Again, only organic and raw, because there's no point in taking in other unknown chemicals, is there?

5. **Get Rid of Acidic Blood:** Most of us have blood on the acidic side, which is necessary for disease, especially cancer. All the processed

foods and sugars, etc. has forced it to be this way. Introduce alkaline immediately to lower the acid level. Fresh greens, seaweed, and many other foods have high alkaline levels, but don't forget to weed out the high-acid foods at the same time, like processed sugar, flours, fats, and bad carbs, and really, most processed, packaged food (alcohol, sauces, and deep-fried--do I even have to say it?) The more processed, the more poison, in most cases! Make your own juice, for instance, because you are probably getting nothing but sugar and chemicals in the juice you're buying. You don't know what chemicals it was grown or processed in. You saw that world news on arsenic in most apple juices, right? There's no way to trace and control what goes into processed foods!

6. **Oxygen:** Disease and cancer also require lack of oxygen to thrive. I realized recently that somewhere in my life, I stopped breathing properly! I usually take shallow, quiet breaths, and I don't inhale or exhale fully. The couple of times a week I'm exercising is not sufficient; it needs to be the majority of the time. I read about the way I should be breathing and seriously, it's work to re-learn it now! It feels great, but I have a lot of practicing to do yet. It's crazy! The fastest way I've found, so far, is a simple 5-minute meditation of just paying attention to my breathing in and out. There's many reasons you hear it so often, "Take a deep breath."

7. **Movement:** The elaborate systems in our bodies can't function properly if it doesn't get enough movement in a day. There are the obvious things

like muscles, but everything else counts on movement too. The lymphatic and circulatory systems can't do their jobs without movement, and wouldn't you agree, they're kind of important? How's the lymphatic system supposed to get rid of the steady, overloaded stream of toxins if we're not moving our bodies enough for them to be active?

8. **Frame of Mind and Spirit:** You've heard me say it before, "The mind has the most power over our bodies and our lives." Truly, what you think you are and what you think will be, will be your life. If you focus on illness, you will have illness. If you focus on health and healing, you will have health and healing. "Ask and Ye Shall Receive" applies to all thoughts, good or bad for you. Keep your blessings, the gift in every person and situation, and clear thoughts of what you want first and foremost in your mind. As you let love and compassion in for yourself, you will automatically extend it to your health and well-being and to everyone around you. Take the time to listen to your heart and soul. It is the core of your being and again, is very much connected to the rest of you!

There's tons of information on all of these things on the internet, and in good books out there, including some basics in RISE ABOVE THE SH**! Down-to-earth thinking from Wisconsin, and in my free articles on health. Truly, we don't write this stuff to make people paranoid; I just can't stand people getting sick and dying when it's so unnecessary! My advice is to KEEP IT SIMPLE and LOVE YOURSELF!

When I have a hard time doing the things that I know are good for me, I try to stop and ask myself, "What do I have against myself, and being happy?" I know, that if I am valuing myself as I should, I would never do anything to harm myself…I would only do things that are good for me. Regardless of any guilt or undeserving-ness I may feel, I try to stop and remind myself of the truth. God creates every person out of pure love, love for each individual and love for the world. No matter what, He wants nothing but love for us and a life of heaven, both now and forever. Only I keep that from myself, when I don't release and heal the things I judge myself for. It's not what God wants. He wants us to forgive and to be compassionate to everyone, and that includes ourselves. Everything starts inside of ourselves. I just try to keep working on it, a little every day; it's a step forward in all ways. Sure is easier when I have my health! :) *~Mary Anne*

MARY ANNE'S SUSPICIOUS MASSES MELTED WITH FRESH-GROUND FLAXSEED?

Health  ***May 2013***

<u>DISCLAIMER:</u> Each of us is beautifully unique, in heart, mind, body, and soul. Therefore, always go with what's best for you. What works for one person may not work for another, but if it's harmless and you think it might work for you, try it out, adjust, or discard if necessary. Only you know YOU! I am not here to give critical advice, only to suggest ideas and to share what works for me. <u>You need to decide what works for you</u>. I do not have ANY medical training; I am merely sharing my experience! We all go through experiences or have someone close to us go through them; I hope this helps, in some way.

First of all, DON'T WORRY! I am totally fine, and always will be! This is the first I'm telling family and friends about my health scare, only because worry is worse than a plague and I know it can kill me! I wasn't even going to tell my boyfriend because I was afraid he'd challenge my thought process or worry. I changed my mind when I got a clear message from above to tell him. I found out then, that he really believed in me and the power of positive thoughts, as he's always telling me, "You'll figure it out; it's just one more journey to write about." Now that I'm letting you in on my secret, I need you all to do the same. Please keep any thoughts about me and anyone else on HEALING and HEALTH, not on any issue or disease, as worry and negative thoughts can literally kill. I had to wait until I had proof I was healing this because I need everyone to stay focused on what I want: Health, Long Life, and Happiness! I want to live a long, long time yet, not because I'm afraid of dying, but because I feel like I have a lot to do for myself, my loved ones, and the world, before this life is over. I've only just begun really living!

So here I go again, sharing what I've learned about breast health issues, only because there's a good chance that most of you will be touched by a similar situation in your life. It's so important to look at all options and stay in control of what happens to your body—it's the only one you get! I shared a lot of basic health information in my book, RISE ABOVE THE SH**! Down-to-earth thinking from Wisconsin, and in free articles since then, but here are some specific things I've learned recently about breast issues. Divine timing stepped in again, with all the health-challenged people that have shared their secrets with me in the last couple of years, so I had a jump-start on all this…there is always a reason. When I told some of you last year I was completely healthy, I really didn't know then, and thought I was healthy…just so you know!

I realized early in 2013, that for months, I'd been more tired and thirsty than usual and my boobs were getting more and more tender. Sharp pains were even waking me up at night, if it was the right time of the month, or if I had too much sugar or caffeine the day before. Heavy and uncomfortable for too long, I decided I better have the doctor check it out. She was immediately concerned, telling me I was more swollen and lumpy than usual, and sent me off for a diagnostic mammogram, even though my last preventative mammo was less than a year old, and was supposedly fine. The mammo appointment turned into consultation with the radiologist and an ultrasound, there on the spot. Everyone was worried and treating me like I had breast cancer, already, because of a suspicious mass or two. I appreciated them all being so kind, but I honestly didn't think I had anything to worry about. It was my body, and I knew I could find the source of the problem and change it, whatever it was. I'm so appreciative I'm learning to pay attention to, and ask God for what I need to know. He sends these strong feelings that bring me peace, all the time.

My primary doctor called as soon as I was back from the mammo to tell me they wanted me to see a surgeon within a few days. The surgeon wanted a biopsy right away, but I thought it was a little extreme, as you'll read below. I told her I wanted to research and asked if any other tests could be run first. So, she sent me in for an MRI with dye to see if it would tell them anything more. In the meantime, I asked for general blood work with my regular doctor, especially checking my hormone levels, but I guess nothing really showed up. There are opinions out there that most doctors don't know about the specific tests to look closely enough for most of the issues with hormones and iodine deficiency, until it's too late and the numbers are ridiculous, but again, everyone has different factors, anyway. Even so, the standard meds aren't necessarily the most effective way to treat it and can cause all sorts of other problems. My primary doctor helped me understand a little more too, that a woman's hormones change constantly, until post-menopause, and they affect pretty much everything, including cholesterol numbers. Two tests, two days in a row can be different, so you can't just go by the tests, sometimes. I told him he was nuts going into medicine, with all the moving parts within the body that affect everything else, with the mind and soul on top of it! But it's all pretty powerful and miraculous, too. Every single body is so unique. But back to my saga. . .

Once the MRI results were back, I went to see the surgeon again and she said she needed to talk to the radiologist yet, but that it looked like they were not overly concerned, and we would just watch it. I was relieved, but still didn't have my questions answered about what was causing the pain, tiredness, lumps and swelling; they really didn't know. That's okay, I will figure it out, I thought. By the time I got home though, I had an urgent message from the surgeon. She apologized, saying the radiologist called right after I left, and in talking to him, she really needed to remove the entire 2cm mass on the left side and see what it was. The lymph nodes nearby were questionable too, so possibly those…but really, I should just come back in and talk about it. All I could hear in my head was a strong message I had gotten repeatedly over the last couple of months, "Get a second opinion!"

Yea, that's right! I still get to decide what I do, with my body, and this just didn't sound right. I would do more research and do all I could to heal it myself. It didn't matter what it was; even if it was cancer, I can still heal it because that's how the body is made. I thought about paying out of my own pocket to get another test, a thermogram, done. My doctor's opinion was that my hormones were very active, so a thermogram would read active, everywhere and it wouldn't help. But even if something did show cancer, I still wasn't willing to go through traditional treatment. I would still want to attempt to heal it on my own, knowing chemo and radiation would only hurt the rest of my body. No, I needed to change whatever was causing it so my body could take care of it, not just try to put a band-aid on every lump that showed up; there could be tons of lumps in there! I cancelled my recall visit with the surgeon to give myself time to see what I could do.

Knowing that I am truly the only one responsible for myself, I asked questions and I did my research, using the internet and books from the library. What causes breast problems? What cures it? What I found kind of ticked me off, to say the least.

<u>Causes:</u> Food and Drink, as I'll go into below (not to mention smoking, which is obvious), Radiation

(including mammograms! WHAT?!! I won't be doing those very often, any more…maybe never!), Iodine Deficiency, and other obvious things that we all know can cause other diseases as well.

Treatment: Nothing has improved, in ages. Cancer IS on the rise, despite all the BS you read that misleads us all, and treatment via chemotherapy and radiation is NOT raising the survival rate, not at all. I believe the traditional treatment itself is often the real cause of death, so really? I refuse to be part of those statistics. Cancer Miracles that I know have a couple of things in common: They DON'T do the traditional treatments, especially chemo and the meds. They research and ask questions and know the side effects. They increase their health and remove toxins from their environments and foods and body. Their focus is on health and surviving.

My Condition: I have fibrocystic breasts (heavy and lumpy), along with probably a third of all women in this country. It makes mammograms, MRIs, ultrasounds, and even a cut-open breast hard to analyze for what is hard breast tissue and what is a foreign mass. It's often a guess. A 2cm mass on the left side worried the doctors enough for them to want to cut it out completely, and maybe the congested lymph nodes next to it. In asking more questions, they'd need to give me a 4-inch scar and they would be guessing where the mass started and ended.

Impact: I had to ask this question, "What if it is cancer, and it's all contained and you accidentally cut into it.

Won't that release cancerous cells into my body?" The doctor only answered that if it was cancer, they'd go in and remove more tissue in the surrounding area, but she knew I didn't like this answer because obviously, the rest of the body is connected and cells move. And again, I'd have a nice scar and probably a deformed breast. It wasn't going to fix anything.

My Instincts: All along I kept getting signs to get a second opinion and change my diet. I was also frustrated by the fact that my right breast hurt much more than the left, and I questioned a big, swollen area the pain was coming from. They also said there was a weird, partially cystic, partially solid mass on that side, but they'd just watch it. Nope, I will not be cut into more than once, and if they can't tell what it is, forget it. I'll work on healing it on my own. The body and mind is the most powerful thing there is to healing disease (especially cancer), so I'll just take care of it myself, as much as I can. Still, my doctor said she wants to know exactly what it is, either way, and says it's best to cut it out. I reassure all doctors involved that I'm not in denial; I just want a shot at healing the source instead of slowly cutting pieces of my boobs out, as the lumps continue. Something made them start hurting all the time in the last few months, and whatever it was, has to go. But what was causing it? I know better than to believe it's just age. Nothing is just age—it's always a build-up or wearing out of something. Were the toxins I've absorbed in my lifetime finally catching up with me? Probably.

<u>What I Did:</u> First, I let myself rest a little more, instead of going out or doing things I really didn't need to do. Keeping my mind and heart on healing was my first priority. Having the energy to research and to ask God for constant strength, faith, and guidance was key. It was trying at times, not to question if I was being wise about this, and did I have what it took to have the faith to heal myself? It was challenging when I was tired or dealing with something negative to not feel like a victim and start feeling sorry for myself. I just had to continue believing that everything happens for a reason, and for a greater good; I had to be patient and allow myself to be guided to whatever was best for me.

I have to admit all along though, that from the beginning, I felt God was telling me, there was nothing to worry about; all would be fine. I've heard Him say this at many scary points in my life, and He's never let me down, so I had no reason to doubt Him. So I laid low for a few months and pretty much eliminated toxins by viewing them as poisons that would feed my lumps. Alcohol, caffeine, and processed foods were rarely touched, and if so, I made sure I was doing lots to detox myself before and after. Negativity had to be cut off at the knees, from any source, including people close to me; I just had to avoid it, all I could, knowing it would directly feed my stress and my health issue. Spirituality is the only way I know to stay focused and strong, and so I made myself follow Divine Guidance and start learning what yoga and meditation and proper breathing is all about. I prayed more and if I was slipping into doubt, I looked for any avenue to pick me back up, including short discussions about it with my boyfriend; it could not be a focus of our time together, just a quick support session, here and there. As I found spiritual experts and energy healers, I looked into them, and if I felt compelled, I met with them. I got lots of meditation CDs from the library on healing. We all need some kind of healing, so what better time to allow it? And boy, did I get my money's worth, from all of it! You wouldn't believe what you uncover and repair, once you just start digging…again, it's ALL CONNECTED to YOU!

I also started in the most obvious place. I'm a pretty healthy eater, really, but I guess I need to get better at it. My boyfriend has been a huge inspiration, the last few months, losing 40 pounds by cutting out a lot of the junk he said I told him about. So now I take the time to think and eat healthier. White, processed things (and yucky processed fats and oils) are poison to the body. <u>Nearly all processed</u> fats, salt, sugar, and flour are nothing but toxic to our bodies, whether you're baking with it or eating or drinking it in a packaged item. Reading labels more and replacing these things with healthier items and cutting back in general, automatically dropped a couple pounds and had me feeling better. Along with this, the more I learn, the more I realize that unless it's fresh, organic, and raw, there are probably more poisons in it than nutrients. Most of America overeats calories full of toxins of all kinds…this is the sad truth, and we wonder why everybody's so sick? So, I've been taking more time grabbing fresh, organic stuff and eat tons of it, because it's all very yummy!

Our tastes buds start to come back as we wean ourselves off the toxic foods and drink, so eventually, you'll taste the difference! (I especially like Dr. Joel Fuhrman's Super Foods list of high-nutrient foods.) Still, with a scary health problem screaming at me, I wanted to do more; this alone didn't seem to be fixing it, fast enough, though it did seem to be lowering my borderline-high cholesterol. I still want to read more of the book, Beat Sugar Addiction Now! by Jacob Teitelbaum, M.D. I'm convinced most of us are addicted to the icky, processed crap, just as the money-makers intended. I believe it's behind the majority of our health problems, I honestly do!

Also, lots of internet research and reading AND warnings from lots of other spiritual and medical sources told me to BREATHE. Did you know that most disease (especially cancer) needs lack of oxygen to survive? Do you realize that most of us don't breathe deeply enough to give our cells all the oxygen they need? It's crazy, but as I started reading and listening to CDs on the proper way to breath, I am re-training my diaphragm and stomach to take in and push out more air. It's clumsy to me right now, but I'm learning. Andrew Weil, MD has some great audios, and he combines very simple meditation, another thing I highly recommend. I won't suggest you do this, but I listen as I'm driving for just a few minutes, sometimes. I have been told by spiritual gurus that my chakras were almost perfectly balanced by this very simple thing. I don't know much about it yet, but I know balanced chakras are cool!

Every tester and doctor I saw asked me how much caffeine I consumed. I have mostly stayed away from caffeine since my early 20s, when my doctor then told me to lay off because it makes my boobs swell a ridiculous amount, and I'd end up with breast cancer, if I didn't. So, I only drank it occasionally, usually in a mixed drink. Once I realized my boobs were hurting all the time, I switched to drinking a little vodka and water, to avoid the soda, and finally, pretty much quit drinking altogether. Why add another toxin, I figure?

Still, my boobs still hurt, at least a little, all the time . . I needed to do more. The breathing and a little meditation would help keep my mind on board and trusting the body could easily heal itself, but I need to go after whatever was causing the fibrocystic build-up to begin with. I didn't care that probably a third of women have this condition. It's not normal, pain is not normal, and it makes me high risk for breast cancer; I didn't have to be a statistic. More research got me back to something I already knew, about how years of toxins make our blood more acidic, and again, most disease needs the acidity to survive. Cancer and many other terminal diseases feast and thrive on sugar, including the extra sugar we give our bodies through all those carbs and condiments we eat. I had cut way back on these things, but wanted to throw some extra alkaline in there to bring it back to where it should be.

God threw it in front of me, as usual. Articles and a talk show led me to buying organic flaxseed and grinding it fresh with a coffee grinder (fresh-ground is the only way to make sure the body absorbs it). There are tons of health benefits (too many to list!) of flax seed when eaten this way, but the articles specifically say that it helps prevent fibrocystic breasts, hormone issues and cancer! I just started using about a teaspoon, and then a tablespoon a day, sprinkled on whatever food I was eating. I had also learned that seaweed (healthy, pure seaweed) is the way to go, and Divine Signs over the last couple of months led me to a raw, organic simple tablet of chlorella/spirulina, known to be able to adhere to, and carry stubborn toxins out of the body, in addition to providing lots of awesome nutrients, including iodine. Lots of health experts claim that in the right form, this combination can cure just about anything.

Oh, iodine! Did you know that nearly all of us are iodine-deprived, especially women? Did you know it causes all kinds of health issues, including hormone imbalance, and that the FDA's recommendations are laughed at by anyone that's researched this? Iodine deprivation can also cause fibrocystic breasts, and is pointed out in lots of articles by wellness experts of the world. I've been on thyroid meds, have struggled with ragging menstrual cycles almost my whole life (in recent years, I routinely get a migraine once a month too!), and not one doctor suggested we look at iodine, but I know, they can't possibly know everything. So just a couple of days ago, after telling my doctor I wanted to try and iodine/iodide supplement, he told me to go ahead and gave me a rough dosage to try. I went out and bought some drops, but returned them without trying them after spiritual guidance told me to just continue eating foods with iodine.

I was fine with that, since the pain and swelling in my breasts disappeared within days of starting the fresh-ground, organic flax seed! Alleluia! Then I get my period, without ANY pain or headache. That NEVER happens, EVER! Something was changing, big time. My energy was returning and my boobs were going back to normal. The lymph nodes were still swollen, but not as much. After less than a month on the flaxseed and only a little longer on the seaweed, I was eager to go to my full physical and have my doctor let me off the hook with this thing!

My primary doctor thought I looked great, despite my normal, lumpy boobs. The swollen lymph nodes still had him questioning if there was something more to pay attention to, though, and he referred me back to the surgeon, saying she was the expert in this area. The problem is, he said, that until you cut it out and examine it, they can't rule out that it's not cancer, and they wouldn't feel comfortable telling me there's nothing to worry about. He answered all my questions and we respected each other's opinions. If your doctor doesn't do this, get another doctor! He also basically told me that I had to understand that I'm a little weird and outside of their normal patients' attitudes, which is to just get unknown growths "out" of them as soon as possible. Yes, he knows me pretty well.

I knew the lymph nodes weren't quite right, and started looking for ways to help my lymphatic system drain. Spiritual guidance and research already helped me understand that sitting and typing all day isn't stimulating my circulation or lymphatic systems at all; I needed to be moving my upper body more often. I'm still working on this, but a couple of simple yoga and dance moves, and just taking the time to raise my hands and arms up a few times a day can't hurt!

The two spiritual healers I met with recently also pegged my physical problem areas right away and went to work on them. I have to emphasize that I don't just run out to every spiritual or energy healer I come across. I'm very fussy and have to be led to them, knowing I'm supposed to be talking to them, before I'll even check them out. Again, only you know what's right for you, and even when the right time is, if ever. What works for me may not work for you at all; ask for guidance from above in everything you need, and it will fall in your lap, at the right time. This is how I found Brian, an energy healer that I knew from his attending one of my speaking events. I didn't know he did this sort of thing until I saw his face in a newsletter of my favorite spiritual store, where he was holding sessions that coming weekend. Of course he had an opening at the only time I could make it, and of course any healing he did of my lymph nodes was just a bonus from all the other issues he helped me clear up. And of course, the lymph nodes shrunk down to almost nothing, by three days later, as I headed out to see the surgeon to see if I could "pass the test." This is how Divine Guidance works, if your faith simply allows it.

Giddy at the start of my second period now with no pain or headaches, and the lymph nodes hard to find, I was excited the day I needed to go back to the surgeon. I envisioned her smiling at me, surprised that all problems had disappeared. I know how powerful my focus is, still, worry tries to stick its ugly head in everywhere. What if I had failed? What if I let my boyfriend down? Would I feel like a fraud, if my mind hadn't been strong enough to know I could heal it? What if she insisted she still had to cut it all out? No, I wouldn't do it. My energy was up, I was feeling great, so despite what anyone said, my problem was GONE. I was the boss of me and it was my decision.

I put my quiet moments to good use all morning. I thanked God for everything in my life, and especially for my health. I asked extra angels to keep me focused and appreciative of life, and to help the surgeon see very clearly, that whatever it was, was now healed. I committed to telling everyone about this, because one little thing in my story could help someone else. Flaxseed, after all, was known to fix many, many things, yet few people know it needs to be fresh and ground, not processed, not whole, not cooked, not old. Organic, fresh and freshly-opened. (I didn't know this until 2 months ago!) If it could do this much to my health, in just a few days, it has to help many other problems as well (for the males out there, too!) I happened to buy brown flaxseed because that's what the grocery store had in organic, and it had an expiration date, so I knew it was fresh. I keep it in the fridge before, and after I grind it, in a small, glass jar. Just like everything else, use in moderation! Don't overdo anything, unless you want to make new problems.

I took an inspirational book along to my appointment, but chose to just pray with my extra waiting time, once I got there. She carefully went over both breasts, from different angles, making sure she no longer had any concerns. She pointed out the two swollen lymph nodes, agreeing that the swelling was way down, and that everything else looked much better now, too. I told her that I was still working on some way to drain the lymph nodes and wouldn't give up until they were. She smiled and said, "Well, looks like it's just a follow-up in 6 months then!" Feeling as if I'd been there before, I didn't even need to respond, other than to tell her that after all I read about the risks of radiation and mammograms, and how they can't really see much through my fibrocystic condition anyway, I really didn't want any more mammograms. I didn't even have to ask; she recommended ultrasound then, which was fine with me.

A happy ending in the surgeon's office, I'm sure, and boy have I learned a lot. I feel very good about knowing the risks of mammograms now (radiation that can fuel breast problems) and will avoid them forever, if possible…they don't make sense for my type of dense breasts (and in a third of you women out there!). I can't even list everything else I learned and am learning now, because of this, on top of all the healing/growing . . . WOW-SA! I don't care if I ever know whether it was nothing, pre-cancerous, or cancer. It doesn't matter. It was draining my energy and causing me pain, and both were only getting worse. I needed to take control and change something. There's no doubt in my mind, that had I not done something, I would have developed cancer. My body did not feel right. I would have been a statistic. I thank God for answering my prayers, once again, of hitting me upside the head so I don't miss things I need to pay attention to. I also have a bigger appreciation for the healthy body I have, and commit to taking better care of it, and stop joking about how I'd like a fresh pair of younger, non-saggy boobs…

So what healed my lumps and swelling and pain? The breathing and meditation? The fresh-ground flaxseed? The positive mindset that I was healed and the spiritual healers? The balancing of the pH in the blood (seaweed)? Reducing the toxins? I'm guessing it's all of the above, and really, I shouldn't stop doing any of them, even if I think it's just any one thing. All of it is great for me and things we all should be doing anyway, so I really don't care what changed it. Clearly knowing I wanted healing leads me to doing the things that will heal me.

The day after the surgeon gave me the green light, I told my sister and Mom the whole story, repeating that I still needed to find a way to fix my lymph nodes, for good. God answered, within a couple of hours. I headed to an easy, low-key yoga class over my lunch hour, and was confused when no one was there? I looked at the schedule on the wall and went to ask the front desk. The woman working, and a customer figured out what was wrong: It was only Wednesday, not Thursday, as I thought! I knew what day it was all morning long, but something totally misled me into going to the gym, thinking it was Thursday. "Oh, but there's a hot yoga class about to start." The receptionist told me. I shook my head, "I don't think I'm ready for that, yet." The customer piped up, "Oh, it's super easy; you could do it. It's just holding poses." I looked back at the receptionist and asked how much the class was, hoping to get out of it. "$7.00, but you can get unlimited hot yoga for $10 a month." The thought of paying to sweat until I passed out didn't intrigue me. Then the receptionist had to throw in, "Oh, but you can do it today, for free, just to see if you like it." The customer looked back at me now, with an encouraging look. Both of them were hoping I'd take the plunge, for some reason. Human angels, again! "Oh, okay, I guess I could try it…" The receptionist ran to get me a free bottle of water too; I was stuck. Turned out, I really liked the class, and as I went through the movements and started to sweat (which I never do), I realized that THIS was definitely going to get my lymphatic system moving—it was all I needed. Funny, God, you sure are something. Thanks for blind-siding me because I would have never done it on my own. Especially a 105-degree, 90-minute class? Thanks for teaching me once again, I can do it!

Throughout this whole ordeal, I knew that once I just trusted everything and stopped doubting and worrying, God would open up my heart, mind, and body to take over and go back to what it does best: SURVIVE and HEAL and FIND PEACE. Our bodies are miraculous machines, and it takes a lot to trip it up, but still, we find more and more ways to pump it full of toxins, every year. I am very sad for the kids that will have very little chance in growing old without a health issue (even via their nervous system, when people miss that it's because of toxins). Add toxic thoughts of worry and stress, not enough breathing and exercise, and you're sure to end up with a disease that will kill you.

Just remember, it's always your choice to be a statistic, or to be the REAL, HEALTHY YOU that God intended you to be. He gives us everything we need. All we have to do is choose what's good for us, not the things that will surely kill us, in one way or another, eventually. Both options are equally available in this fine, leisurely, information-filled country of ours, so don't let lack of self-love hold you back. Other people are counting on you, remember? I try to remind myself, every day! :) Wishing you a long, healthy, peaceful life! *~Mary Anne*

SILLY THINGS THAT GET ME STUCK

Awareness **June 2013**

I dedicate this article to all the beautiful people that came out to see me in New Holstein at Massage Therapy by Mickaela Summers and Valerie Hickman on June 18th; it was such a pleasure to just be with all of you, and I was raring to finish up this article, the next day, and post the picture I took, right after I left there, at my favorite spot in Pipe…it reflects exactly how you all made me feel! I will focus on all of us meeting again! :)

So lately, life feels a little BLAH. There's no reason for it; everything's great and I've met or reconnected with a lot of wonderful people lately, too. So a couple of days ago as I went to bed, I took my own advice and asked, "What am I missing, lately?" I know from experience, that if I want to know the answer to something, I just ask with faith before I go to sleep, and my subconscious mind will work on it all night and provide the answer, as I wake up. The neighbor's outside alarm went off about 4am the next morning, and groggy as I was, I felt like I was on the verge of getting my answer. Still, I had gone to bed pretty late, and wasn't ready to get up, so I decided to go back to sleep, asking God to help clear my mind of whatever sticky fog was clogging it.

It worked. I woke up at 5am and 6am, wondering if it was time to get up yet, realizing I was slowly getting my answers. I was pointed towards looking at what I've been thinking and talking about lately. Despite all the wonderful things going on in my life, and in the lives of those I love, somehow I've been distracted by the not-so-wonderful things. I got thinking about why I haven't been taking a walk every day, this last week. I've been more tired. Why? I've been going to bed late. Why? Mmm. There's been a little negativity creeping in lately, here and there. Even just sprinkled in, every other day or so, it was weighing down my wings.

As I tell my Grandson, "You were born to fly, and don't ever forget it!" Even though he's not even a year old yet, he gets it; I know, because of the gigantic smile on his face. See, we were all born knowing this, and no one's corrupted him yet; at least not on Grandma's watch! So in my human silliness, I have not been flying lately. Oh, good things are all around me, really they are, everywhere I look. That's not the issue. The issue is with the "other" little things that sneak in. The news was on one night, and I paid attention to the awful things going on with people. I took the time to read some sad tributes on Facebook. People I know tell me about the emotional and physical struggles of people we care about. I hear someone speak out in anger against someone. Something reminds me of someone that wronged me, in the past. Some of my fears that block my dreams start to creep out, looking for a place to set up camp. Suddenly, SH** has me surrounded, somehow!

This is all so typical, isn't it? It was the way my life used to be. You trudge along and trudge along, overjoyed by a day that happened to go your way, because it just wasn't an everyday thing. Oh, I remember. My memories of BLAH days are the entire reason I usually work on keeping my head where it belongs, every day. So it hits me aside the head again. My head is not where it belongs to see things clearly, not at all! I've got all this negative stuff that I've been absorbing blocking my view, and my path. Sure, all the negative stuff is always there. The difference lately is that I've been FOCUSING on it, instead of all the positive things I should be focusing on. I've even repeated or added to some of the negative conversation—YUCK! Even if I wasn't naming names, I was talking or thinking about sad or messed-up situations, which only spreads the negativity as more focus is placed on it. I hadn't taken the time to let the SH** just flow by. I had chosen to step in it! No wonder I feel so BLECKY lately!

So thank you God, for helping me see, it's time to step back out of it! I remember now, that all I have to do is REPLACE THE NEGATIVE WITH SOMETHING POSITIVE. It's so flippin' easy, it's a shame I wasted a few days of precious life, really it is! So here's what I do. I include the sad and sick and struggling people in my daily prayers. I ask God and the Angels to help all of them find comfort and healing in God; there's no better feeling than realizing you're never alone and that God's love is overwhelming. I do the same for any news within earshot, immediately going to a prayer instead of analyzing the details of what happened, or how people must feel. My dwelling on it in a negative way does no good, but a prayer brings power and relief to everyone involved. I visualize happiness, health, and peace for all, including me.

For those sneaky little fears that tell me to worry that I am trying to do more than I can handle and that I'm not getting enough done, I push them back into their dark corner by reminding myself that good things are unlimited; all I need to do is ask. So that's another thing I've been missing…naming off specifically what I'm thankful for, instead of thinking or talking about something unpleasant. When I think about what I want and what I'm grateful for, it's important to take a minute to feel happy and at peace, along with all the other wonderful feelings. Here's an example: "Thank you God, for the abundance of love, happiness, health, time, resources, and opportunities to fulfill my dreams and the dreams of my loved ones. Together, I know that nothing is impossible and I accept all of the miracles and goodness in my life."

You see, no matter what it is, good or bad, we still have the CHOICE TO ACCEPT IT. Good or bad, we can embrace it, or turn it away. Sadly, the worldly corruption often makes us feel like we don't deserve things, or that we have to suffer, and so, WE OFTEN

WILLINGLY ACCEPT THE BAD AND TURN AWAY THE GOOD! It's CRAZY, don't you think? Start practicing ACCEPTING THE GOOD! IT'S OKAY! YOU are the reason God put it here! From the sun and the moon, to every person you come in contact with, really! It is for you! Just try it all out, accepting the good, and let yourself be surprised by all the great things that can come out of you, once your head is back where it belongs!

Another thing I'm doing today…right now, as a matter of fact, is TAKING THE TIME TO DO THINGS THAT FEED MY POSITIVE SIDE, like getting outside and taking a short walk! Nature rejuvenates you, happily off-loading all the negative crap you've been storing up. So does uplifting music, and any way that you express your happiness, like singing, saying, writing, or thinking something positive, or any kind of movement, like exercise and dancing. Taking care of your body is the ultimate positive embrace, so I'll make the time to choose good food and drinks today, especially lots of plain water! Do you see how simple it is? Our own happiness lies in all the things we do (and think) for ourselves; the hordes of wonderful people all around me couldn't clear away the pool of SH** I was allowing to rise around my ankles. Great people were in my presence, every day, yet I still felt groggy and not completely alive. As some of the world experts proclaim, "The door to your happiness opens in." So, no more BLAH! (And thank you, God, for helping me to remember this faster, the next time my human-ness gets in my way!) *~Mary Anne*

WHY AM I SO HAPPY? (WHAT'S WRONG WITH ME?)

Awareness  ***July 2013***

People ask me more and more, these days, "Why the heck are you so happy all the time?" I'm glad somebody said something, because I honestly hadn't realized it was that noticeable. Then again, I do know that everything about us, absolutely affects everyone around us. Just knowing this helps to keep me in check. In fact, I'm hoping that most of us would rather leave a path of light for others, as opposed to a path of SH**, wouldn't we? Keep this in mind, as you move through your day!

So am I on something? Is it a man in my life? Is it money? No, No, and Nope! We know those things can never make us deep-down happy. They might distract us for a while, giving us the false impression that we are escaping whatever makes us unhappy, but they really don't; we still know there's a big piece of us missing, without that soul-soaring happy.

I set out to find that big piece I felt I was missing. I just knew there had to be more to this life. In everything I've ever known about how loving God is, I just couldn't accept that I was here to suffer so that I'd be ready for something else. Does anyone that loves anyone want to see them suffer? It's just the opposite, isn't it? Love is about happiness and fulfillment and peace, and that's all God is: Love.

So all I did was pray and ask, "What am I missing, and what is this life really for?" In God's only style, I got way more than I can still comprehend. The wheels of life started turning, big time, because I had finally allowed them to move. Yea, I feel a little slow, taking almost half my life, but I am human, and better late than never, right? Inspiration and understanding of day-to-day challenges came so strongly that I was pretty much forced to share it in the form of my first book, RISE ABOVE THE SH**! Down-to-earth thinking from Wisconsin. If I could save a few people a few years of trudging through the crap, I would feel better about starting so late in my life, I think? Besides, it hit me aside the head, as the answer to all my immediate dreams, so I had no choice.

The more you open up your heart, the more you want to learn about yourself and your life, only because it feels like what I think heaven must be like. Once you get a taste of this, you will do whatever it takes to avoid going back to the old way of living; the old way of living feels like a past life, and maybe it is? Can you imagine the high in leaving all fears, hurts, pains, and unhappiness behind for good? It makes anybody happy enough to almost etch a smile right on to your face! I'm elated to know that my excitement over life is showing. For the first time in my life, I don't mind a little attention. For the first time in my life, my urges to share what I do to be happy are stronger than any fears that wanted me to hide from the judgment of others, the first half of my life. I know that helping even one person find their happiness is worth it, because that one person will impact many others in a good way, including me, somehow. I tell ya, happy and at peace is where it's at!

So I continue to write about what I know, I'm starting to do more public speaking to share what's in my heart, and do my best to get people thinking with these short articles. So let's use the big trend of all the "CLEANSES" to summarize the key things that I think help me. Now any little thing you do helps, and the more you do, the happier you will be, so you decide where to start and how much you will allow for yourself…we all have our own pace. If you aren't happy every day, it's a sign you need to pick up the pace! You aren't getting any younger. Age alone won't kill you, but lack of cleansing will get us all, eventually…so let's get started, keeping in mind that all of these things are connected to each other, so they all work together and absolutely affect you, no matter how much you want to deny it. Cleansing helps you remove the layers of junk to get closer to the real you. The more you are being the real you, the happier and more fulfilled you will be—it's that simple!

CLEANSING OF THE MIND: How much of what's in your head are your true thoughts, and how much was put there by someone else? If it warms your heart and makes you feel at peace, it's yours; if not, it belongs to someone else and needs to go. It's not part of the real you. There's a 15-minute video on my **TeensRiseAbove.com** site that explains how to tell what belongs to you. Just click on the words, "You Are Here For A Reason" in the upper-right-hand corner there. Also, the RISE ABOVE book is all about thinking through the things that are probably someone else's thoughts and about creating your own thoughts on all the common things we stumble on, in a typical day. Yes, you do have full control over your choices and your life, and no, no one else is to blame for where you're at. Accepting responsibility for yourself is like a major power-washing of that gunky window you've been trying so desperately to look through.

Every day, stay focused on what you want, never what you don't want, especially anytime you are lying in bed. List off what you're grateful for. Imagine yourself living your dream life, feeling at peace with everyone around you, in the present moments. What would you and others be doing? How does it make you feel? Even when something blind-sides you, replace any negative thoughts you have with positive, understanding, loving thoughts; you are damaged the most by your own negative thoughts, so clean them out!

CLEANSING OF THE BODY: Thoughts that belong to others dump crap into our heads: "I'm not worth it," or "it's too hard or doesn't matter," or "it won't kill me—it's safe," or a whole assortment of excuses for not taking better care of ourselves. Truly, the source of the reason we don't take care of ourselves is connected to lack of self-worth, which again, comes from other people's thoughts, not our own. The fact that you were born makes you deserving of everything good. If you have even a smidgen of the self-love you should have, you will automatically take better care of yourself. Every little bit of putting less bad stuff in, and more good stuff in makes a huge difference. No brainer, right?

It's so bad in this country, that lack of proper maintenance of our bodies is the #1 cause of death! It's very hard for me to swallow, some days…all we have to do is apply a little common sense to what we do to the only vehicle that will carry us through our lives, in the physical condition that allows us to enjoy the years we have. So, doctors literally save us at several points in our lives, but please realize they are not personally responsible for your health, only about 10% of it, if that. The other 90% is for you to take care of, because again, no matter what you have going on, your body is a miraculous machine, created to heal itself when it is properly maintained. The problem is, the majority of us downright abuse our bodies, because once again, we don't make the effort to think things through and we let the rest of the world tell us what to do. Guess what? A lot of the rest of the world is warped and doesn't care if something is making you sick, or even killing you, if they are making a buck off of it…really, they don't. So why hand your life over to them?

<u>Breathing:</u> There's a reason you keep hearing about taking deep breaths and I highly recommend we all do it,

as many times a day as we can remember. Not only does our body need more oxygen to combat all the crap in our bodies, but stress and everything else has us forgetting how to breathe. When you breathe in, does your belly expand outwards on all sides, and push up your diaphragm, chest, and collarbone? When you breathe out, do you squeeze your belly button into your spine? Can you control and hold the flow of air? If not, you are probably depriving your body of clean air and cutting years off of your life, for real. Cancer and disease relies on lack of oxygen in the body, and we are handing it right over. This aspect of a good yoga class was my sole motivation to finally getting into yoga; I recommend going to an instructor that helps you re-learn how to breathe and coaches you through breathing along with the movements.

<u>What We Consume:</u> I have an assortment of articles now, explaining why so many common foods, drinks, medicines, etc. will shorten your life and even kill you. Seriously, where do you think illnesses come from, when a healthy body is designed to tackle anything it's exposed to? Poison the body directly, or by not giving it anything close to the nutrients it needs and it'll run like a car you are fueling up with sand, water, or anything other than good fuel. Remember, the fresher, the finer, the more processed, the more poison. Please look at the organic options when you shop to minimize the poisons! Please take a look at the carb and sugar content of everything (it'll surprise you!) and remind yourself that cancer and most diseases thrive on the excess glucose and acid in the body! Regarding actual drastic cleanses

though, I wouldn't personally shock my system with most of those; I can't believe it's good for the body at all! Listen to your body!

What We Absorb: Remember that your skin is full of holes and is a major entrance into the body. EVERYTHING you put on your skin is absorbed into your body. Very few of these things are without toxins, including lotion, soaps, shampoos, makeup, cleaners, detergents, etc. Realize it is another battle for your body to constantly fight, along with the unseen energies of negativity, electronics, etc. I believe it's not usually one thing on its own, but the combination of all the toxic armies that eventually wear a weak spot into our bodies. Eventually, the body just can't detox or repair itself fast enough and we manifest a health issue to force us to pay attention to it, and ideally, to change something to give the body a fighting chance. Listen to your body. Listen to your truth. You can change what you're doing immediately!

CLEANSING OF THE HEART/SOUL: Every day, I try to pray that I keep myself open to everything God sends my way, so that I can learn more about myself and have a positive impact on others. I ask Him to guide me and keep my awareness sharp, so I don't miss anything. (I ask Him to hit me aside the head, and He often does, but I have to laugh—He's got quite a sense of humor :) This requires learning and growing and healing and forgiving and understanding and compassion, just to get started. It does require effort, and bearing one's soul often digs up pain and fear that was buried long ago, but relief comes quite quickly when we embrace it and heal the deepest scars we have. Moving through it brings peace and courage, and honestly, is much easier to live with than the unhappiness I felt I couldn't control. Fulfillment comes as we start to realize how amazing we really are, when we do our best to lead with our hearts and shine with our souls; it's truly the only thing I believe we're really here to do. There are countless ways to actively acknowledge this critical piece of you; any positive learning or activity or people will move you closer. Remind yourself that any little positive thing you do for your mind, body, or heart/soul is an expression of self-love; practice, practice, practice! I ask for guidance daily through prayer, meditation, nature, learning, and mindfulness, knowing everything and everybody happens for a reason.

Above all, I strive to live as many moments as I can in "Never, Never" Land.

NEVER listen to your ego/fears/doubts/lies/mind viruses over your heart and true self, and

NEVER take on anyone else's SH** (in the form of thoughts, limitations, judgments, beliefs, feelings, etc.)

Basically, if something or someone is not nurturing your highest, loving self, consider doing some cleaning . . . remember, everything is affecting you in a good way, or a bad way, at all times, so use your free will to CHANGE your life now. You are losing valuable moments that you will never have again. Every day, you are one day closer to the end of your life here, I can guarantee that! Any fears you have of change are only from not choosing to live in "Never, Never" Land, as I've explained above. The real truth is, CHANGE allows you to move forward and to grow. I think of CHANGE this way:

"**C**hoose **H**appiness **A**nd **N**otice **G**ood **E**verywhere"

The good is there, everywhere . . . a little cleansing will help you to see it more clearly every day, until people start wondering, "What's wrong with you? Why are you so happy?" Yea, you can't help but smile at that, so smile and be happy, and as a day with my friends Jo and Jessie inspired me to say, "Put your cheeks into it!" : #
~Mary Anne

SICK? DON'T BOTHER READING THIS UNLESS YOU REALLY WANT TO GET BETTER

Health  ***August 2013***

Lately, it seems like I'm surrounded with news of people with advanced cancer and mysterious, crazy, deadly diseases. Many are hopeless, as they rely on the doctors, and are slowly (and sometimes, not so slowly) inching closer to leaving us. It's hard to watch, and it makes me sad, because as people are overwhelmed with the seriousness of it, they look to the doctors to be their God in healing them, and don't seem to look beyond. The sad truth is, doctors can only help us with 10% of what we need to heal; the other 90% needs to come from us, and possibly, from other healing experts, in some cases. This is not my thought, it's a proven fact. We need to stop giving doctors all the responsibility; they are human, just like we are. They are not God, and usually cannot perform miracles.

Another truth is, cancer and other deadly diseases (some that they can't even name and understand yet) ARE on the rise, and no, the cures are NOT on the rise. Some cancer research charities will word things to lead you to believe otherwise, but read the real facts, and you'll see things ARE getting worse. Why? For a lot of obvious reasons, mostly going back to the fact that we are slowly poisoning ourselves and not giving our bodies what they need. Convenience in food and drinks load us up with poisons, to the point our bodies are overloaded and cannot function properly, which means it gets behind on healing anything that comes along, as a normal body would. Belief that nothing else affects our health also has us running in the wrong direction and slowly killing ourselves, literally.

Again, I don't make this SH** up; there is scientific proof behind all of it, which you easily find, if you do your homework. As always, be wise enough to read between the lines of proof and opinion, and use your own common sense in finding things to try, to help yourself or a loved one. If 10 world experts say that studies show proof of something working or not working, but then you read one article that says, "there's no proof that plastic causes cancer," for instance, don't cop out with an excuse for not trying something new that might help. In other words, get rid of the plastics that have been proven to be harmful and start using glass to store and heat foods up in the microwave! It's way too easy to have any excuses in not trying it, especially if you're sick. Why on earth would you risk putting more poison in your body, when such a simple change can reduce the risk? Again, you have to ask yourself, do I really want to be healthy?

So here's what I know, so far, and I hope you take these things seriously, if you seriously want to get better, or help a loved one get better. What have you got to lose, at this point? Try everything that could possibly help and not cause additional harm! You don't know how much time you have!

MINDSET: It's a proven fact that what you believe, deep down, is what you will get. There are plenty of books explaining this, but it's as sure as there's oxygen in the air we can't see, but still need. There is measurable energy in all the systems of our body, including the brain and heart. FYI, the heart produces the most energy of all. So guess what? If deep down in your heart, you feel that life is hard and you're tired of all the things in your life, you are sending out a HUGE message (YES, in the form of measurable energy) that you'd rather not be here, with all the struggle. I hate to be the one to point out, that whatever you think, deep down, has to come about eventually, including an exit to a life that is considered too hard to be worth it. Don't do it, unless you mean it! IF you have been thinking this way, it's time to clean up your thinking, NOW! Replace your toxic thoughts with a commitment and focus on taking care of yourself and on healing. You cannot heal, unless you believe you can heal and set that as your deep-down desire. There just may be people around you that don't want to lose you yet!

CONNECTIONS: Your body is all one unit, right? So guess what? If it's all stuck together, it is ALL STUCK, together! Anything that goes on in one system or part of your body is absolutely affecting something else in your body. In the case of nutrition, toxins, and breathing, it's affecting EVERY PART of your body. Thinking medicine or treatment only impacts one part of your body is complete BS; come on, think about it! Again, is your heart and mind part of your body? So yes, what it believes and truly wants, deep down, DOES affect everything. If you still don't want to believe this, I highly recommend you start learning more about it and decide for yourself, instead of just going with a silly belief that someone else has, that never seriously took the time to learn about it, including doctors. Doctors are amazing and have saved me and my loved ones more than once, but remember, they are human, and how the heck can one human have the time or capacity to know everything? And how do you expect another person to know more about what's going on in your mind, body, and soul, than you do, anyway? They are NOT responsible for you—YOU ARE! Take responsibility for yourself. Playing the victim won't get you anywhere. You are still in charge, whether you admit it, or not. Again, don't mess around with this; no one is guaranteed another day in their life. No one.

NUTRITION AND LACK OF NUTRITION: The most heart-breaking to me of all, is the total disregard we have for what we consume. Just because someone's selling it, it doesn't mean it's safe, or of any good to our bodies, at all. Our bodies are alive and NEED GOOD FUEL! If we don't give ourselves the nutrition we need, the body cannot function properly, and you're gonna get sick. If you stick more poisons in than nutrition, you will eventually kill yourself. It's really quite simple, I think. Again, why would you poison yourself, and makes excuses like, "They can't prove it causes cancer," or "It's not gonna kill me." Really? How do you know that? Sure, maybe once, twice, or 200 times, your body can detoxify it and flush out the crap you're putting in, but what happens when you put in hundreds of poisons, or get to the 201st time you ate or drank that poison, and your body just can't take it anymore? What do you think is gonna happen? And what do you think it's fighting it with, when you don't eat, drink, or breathe properly? Invisible nutrients and oxygen? Don't LIKE the healthy stuff? Guess what? You're in trouble, because all the toxins have your taste buds all messed up and you're probably addicted to several chemicals, just like a person gets addicted to the well-known drugs out there. As you heal your addictions by getting away from the toxic foods and drinks and introducing healthy stuff, your taste buds will eventually return to normal, so that you can taste how good fresh food is. Find a way. Mask the high-nutrient foods, like spinach and carrots, by making yourself a smoothie or juice with your favorite fruit, and hiding it in there. Juicing is very healing because the more you break open live plant cells, the more your body can use them. (That's one reason you're supposed to chew things up finely.) Just stick to organic greek yogurt in your smoothies (without a ton of added sugar!) and organic fruits and vegetables, because you really don't need the extra toxic chemicals that can be in non-organic stuff, do you? Give your poor body a break, and feed it well. It's DYING for good fuel to function! Can your car run on water in the gas tank? What makes you think your body can run without proper fuel, then? Can I point out that your body is a slightly more sophisticated and complicated machine, than a car? Can I remind you, it's the only one you got?

TOXINS: Have no doubt, the rise in cancer and disease is absolutely from the overload of toxins. Lack of nutrition and mindset make it almost impossible to detoxify from all the crap that we're exposed to, every single day. Air quality sucks, in most of the country, and most of us don't take a deep breath, hardly ever, so we're NOT getting sufficient oxygen anyway; the cells in our bodies NEED oxygen. Cancer and disease THRIVE when we are not breathing properly. Most of the body, household, and especially outdoor products are LOADED with poisons that we inhale, absorb through the open pores of our skin, and even consume, somehow. (Like plastic poisons, from water bottles and food containers.) You already know that your body counts on plain, toxin-free water to clean out toxins, right? I have not found very many low-toxin-risk drinks out there at all, so I usually stick to plain water, organic milk, or a freshly-squeezed, organic juice. I don't miss the soda or sugar-and-chemical-loaded juices at all. They are not worth bringing back the allergies, body aches, or tumors I used to have.

TRY, TRY, and TRY AGAIN: If you really want to live a long, happy life, why not take the time to do your own research, on your particular ailments, and connect with others that have cured it? When I developed breast tumors and lymph node problems, I had one thought in mind: Find the source and change something to stop it from feeding the tumors. I knew that the tumors were my red flag that my body was struggling with something that I could correct. I didn't let the doctors take a biopsy because it could absolutely spread the cells of the tumor. What good would it do, anyway? I either had cancer or pre-cancerous tumors, according to everything I researched. Either way, I just wanted to stop it in its tracks and heal it, not risk spreading it. It didn't take me long to find a list of plants that are PROVEN to kill cancer cells. PROVEN! Yet when I asked my doctors, they really didn't know about it. Again, we have to remember, doctors are geniuses, trained in the specifics of proving quick fixes to keep us alive, usually by treating the one thing. We have to be responsible in making the decisions, like the impact on the rest of our body. I eliminated soda and most alcohol and added organic, fresh-ground flax seed to my diet, and BANG! Within a few days, my tumors were gone. GONE! People I know have added some of the other cancer-killers, like turmeric and aloe vera, in addition to the flax seed, and have told me they feel cured as well. Again, stick with ORGANIC and FRESHLY ground or squeezed. I found that my flax seed is ineffective if it's older than about 5 days ground. There is something out there that can help. Keep looking!

I've written lots more in other articles, providing specifics on some of these things, so please take a look and pass it on to the people you care about. There's lots more easy-to-access information out there, too, and I recommend you start with the Super Foods to start fueling up with the stuff that your body needs to heal. And drop the toxins like soda, right away. Again, it's proven that a change in nutrition and attitude can heal ANYTHING. ANYTHING! This stuff is so simple. Why are people saving it as a "last resort?" Why do people take on treatments that are killing them to the point that nothing can save them, at that point?

Wouldn't it be a lot easier, cheaper, and effective to just start with the basics of health? It kind of kills me that they call the stuff that really works "ALTERNATIVE MEDICINE". . . but it kills me more that people don't think they're worth taking the time to look at the proven facts of what does and does not work. They just take on some random opinion of someone that doesn't know a thing about it, instead of talking to the experts in that area of "ALTERNATIVE MEDICINE." Makes me think that people just don't think they're worth it, and again, it makes me very sad. I really don't want to see one more person kill themselves through a slow death of toxins, so please give this some serious thought and do what YOU THINK makes sense, not what you think someone else thinks. It's your body, and it's your life. Don't put anyone else in charge of it! *~Mary Anne*

WHY ISN'T LIFE GETTING ANY BETTER?

Letting Go  ***September 2013***

Look, it's really so much simpler than we make it. Until we get out of the heart-set that we are a victim of others, and really, of life, and start realizing we are truly the only ones that drive our life, life cannot give us everything we want! Start driving and quit waiting! All the frustration I see with the wait-ers breaks my heart . . . if they only knew how close they are…haven't they had enough?

So if you've read any of my other articles, or my RISE ABOVE THE SH**! Down-to-earth thinking from Wisconsin book, this is not the first time you've heard me say it. If you know me personally, you have heard story after story (some rather miraculous) of how my thoughts and actions have me living my dreams, more and more, all the time. It blows my mind; I could never have imagined all the good that is present, every day I remember I am not random, not a victim, and certainly not anyone that has to wait for anything to happen "to me." Trust me when I say, I'm not bragging . . . I am merely trying to help others reach out that extra inch, knowing how much that little effort has changed my life!

Now, if you haven't read my other articles, I want to set the record straight right now. My miracles come from living from my heart, as much as humanly possible. I do my best to thank God every day, to ask Him only for what I want, and to live a positive life style where I put effort into learning to love unconditionally, starting with myself. I know that I am here for a reason and that my level of true happiness absolutely impacts the rest of the world. God created us all for this reason, and there is no limit or lack of happiness available to any of us, it is only our own "buts" that keep us from it.

So as I started writing this at 1:11 am in the morning because I haven't been sleeping much at all lately, I am not focused on the inability to sleep. Instead, I have learned to ask myself honestly, "What is my heart trying to tell me? What am I ignoring?" The body doesn't just decide not to sleep; it is designed to sleep. A healthy mind, body, and soul has no problem sleeping, but when it needs our attention, it will try anything to get it. Sometimes we get sick. Sometimes we encounter people and situations that we could really be much happier without. Sometimes we lie awake at night. Sometimes we wonder what life is all for? PAY ATTENTION! You are desperately trying to get through to you, but you have put something in the way of your happiness.

We are our own, and usually our ONLY enemy. We literally put our own butt in the way of our happiness, in the form of "buts." Be honest--do you ever let any of these evil thoughts creep in? You WILL get what you think about!

→ But they (or it) won't let me…
→ But I can never get ahead…
→ But they (or it) is making me unhappy…
→ But I don't have time, or I have to wait until…
→ But I need this, to do that…
→ But this happened to me…
→ But I have this health issue…
→ But something always happens; it never works out…
→ But I can't or I don't know how…
→ But I don't deserve it/them…

Oh my! Such a bunch of crap, but I know as well as you do, it's pretty hard to identify it as crap, when you can't see through the thick stuff! Like I used to be, it's probably all you know of this life, so far, but trust me on this one . . . a little retraining never hurt anyone, so please take a minute to read on. Living from the heart is very, very simple. **With anything you think, do, or say, ask yourself, "Is this doing me, my heart, and my life good? Do I jump for joy over this, even when I think about it later on?"** If your answer is YES, then you are being true to yourself, your life, and you are on the right path for you! If your answer is NO, then you need to change something, and it's most likely, the way you think and what you are not doing for yourself. If your answer is I DON'T KNOW, then you need to ask yourself why you're afraid to give yourself an honest answer and work on loving yourself enough to start being honest with yourself!

Now, when it comes to other people and what they say or do to you, the same holds true. If it warms your heart and makes you feel great, every time you think about it, it is part of the true you. But if it hurts you, makes you feel unworthy, disconnected, and makes you want to close off your heart, it's something that needs to be identified as BS, or something that needs to be healed or released from your life. Realize that negative events, illness, and even people will continue to surface as long as you do not attempt to heal or change whatever comes with them, as a way to force you to pay attention to this "but." I hope that someday, you can appreciate even the most negative people and events you've ever come across, as a great teacher of how to overcome one or more of your "buts." Learn more about yourself, remember there is a reason for everything, learn the lesson, and move on to bigger, better, and SO much happier things!

Second, please realize that EVERYTHING you think, do, or say either **HELPS** or HARMS you and your life . . . EVERYTHING! There is no in between. You are alive and life is moving! Do not feed the "buts!" It takes so much more energy, time, and even your health, to feed the "buts!" Start setting a new standard of loving yourself by doing things that HELP you:

TAKE THE TIME, EVERY SINGLE DAY, to think and feel the joy of your dream life, no matter where you're at now…no "buts" allowed! Keep the thought POSITIVE, only thinking about what you want, NEVER what you don't want. Big or small, it all counts, just start doing this now, in some way! Surround yourself with only those things that feed your dreams!

FIND SOME KIND OF SPIRITUALITY! You have a spirit, and every day, you are either nurturing it or draining it. There are just way too many options and active churches, groups, and accepted practices these days to have any excuse of not being spiritual, in some way. Think long and hard . . . you know that you know you have a soul . . . start listening to it!

CHANGE ANYTHING YOU ARE NOT HAPPY WITH, PERIOD! Do it your own way, trying everything until something works, but change it! Habits, addictions, beliefs, the way you feel about yourself, daily routines, and even the people you hang out with should change as it no longer helps your life. We are meant to learn and grow our entire life, and move forward our entire life, and it automatically contributes good to the world, when we do! Don't look at anything as a mistake, unless you keep repeating it once you realize it is not helping you. You're human. Recognize what needs to change and do your best—your honest best—to show yourself a little love! You can do anything with your "but" out of the way!

Please find a little love for yourself and try out something . . . anything, that this article may have stirred in your heart, even if it's to read another free article or two on a topic that interests you. Start anywhere, but just start! As I tell people in my workshop, I can absolutely guarantee that after today, you are one step closer to being through with this life. You are one day closer to being dead, so what the hell are you waiting for? LIVE WHILE YOU ARE HERE! *Much Love, ~Mary Anne*

DEATH IS NOT THE END

Relationships 

October 2013

I was going to save this sensitive topic for my next book, but a number of recent tragic deaths presses me to blurt it out now. I sincerely believe I was touched by all this for a particular reason and I thank God that it's obvious to me now; I can possibly bring a little more peace to myself and others by writing from my heart about this. That's true any time, any place. Anything from the depth of your heart is always good for you and good for others; there's no going wrong in that.

It all started when the news came of 3 local, sudden deaths in just a few days' time; everyone scattered to try to reach out to their loved ones. For the first time in my life, I said, "Thank God for Facebook." It made it easy to talk to those left behind and know they were hanging on, and I saw heart-written post after post after post by those closest to those that had gone, as well as those trying to comfort them. I doubt I will ever see so much love and honesty in social media, ever again! I felt very blessed, just witnessing it, and to see all the happy photos everyone was sharing. Thousands had to have been touched by it!

As I was about to go to sleep the night I heard about the second death, I asked God what I could do, to help all those hurting so badly? I also thought of the loneliness stirring as others were reminded of their dearly departed, regardless of how long it'd been. Praying is powerful, and all I could do, at the time. I felt a deeper peace when I woke up in the middle of the night with thoughts of what one might say to their loved ones, left behind, and the words just flowed from my fingers to the screen, without any forethought. I have learned not to hesitate or even think about it for a moment, as this is where my best writing comes from. I merely act as a transcriptionist in sending messages out to whomever they are intended for. Again, this works for everyone. Following a nudge from the heart is always good. And so, inspired by all the heart-felt words stringing across the Facebook pages, I posted the result, a poem titled, "Thank You For All the Tears," praying the grieving loved ones would see it.

One by one, I attended services for each, hoping a hug or a look or a prayer would bring comfort to all in grief. At times, I told myself to stop smiling so much, as some may be very confused. You see, I tend to dwell on the wonderful things about the person or their loved ones, out of gratitude for having known them, or knowing of them through someone I care about. Everyone has something important to teach us, and even if you don't know the deceased, you learn a lot about them from everyone at their funeral. It also fills me with joy to think of the wonderful things the deceased must be experiencing, as they move on to the next phase of their eternal life; even if it's an immediate return to earth, as some believe happens in the case of suicide. No matter what, they have a new beginning and a new chance to continue learning about divine love. To me, it's all good; all we need to do is be happy for them, too.

The only thing that brings tears to my eyes is the sadness in the others at the service; I want so badly to help them know, without a doubt, their loved one is safe in divine love. How can I be so sure? Well, for one thing, all limitations of our human form are gone, and without that, all that's left is the spirit, the soul, or the heart's pure love. It is crystal clear that everyone's core is divine and pure love; it's only the physical form that disguises and misleads everyone. Once that's shed, we remember our true existence and I believe, it uncovers the true existence of everyone left behind for the deceased to see, and so, the deceased knows that everyone always did the best they could. There are no hard feelings, nothing but love. I know this may be hard to comprehend, but maybe that's why most of us can't experience it until we do leave this world? We can only have faith and try our best to understand.

So if you can believe that we are eternal, you can acknowledge our core existence: Our souls. Any deep connection we have with others is at the SOUL level, truly, not just a physical level, right? However you want to look at it, whether it be our hearts, souls, or spirits, the lasting, caring connections stem from these, not just a physical body, right? A look, a knowing, any sharing of emotion, any of the good stuff, we know, comes from the heart/soul/spirit. We just know. So do you see where I'm going with this yet?

When we feel blindsided by life, the usual human fears, regrets, egos, and personal demons jump on board and do their best to drown out the heart, and cover up the truth. It's easy to let them take over when there's nothing but sorrow. When someone is out of their heart, it becomes easy to be out of their mind, as well. Their internal misery is sometimes expressed in some very unhealthy and even nasty ways, both self-induced and in outward attacks on others. We all need to remember, negativity is nothing more than expression of internal misery, regardless of whether the miserable person ever realizes it, or not.

But most times, the result is overwhelming grief over the loss; this is where I never mean to offend anyone suffering with my smiles, but wish so badly I could lead others to this place. The physical loss of the body of someone we love does not touch the soul connection we have with this person. Sure, the physical presence of this person was awesome, but the intensity of it was because of the SOUL connection you have with them. I mean, think about it. You're around other people all day long that you never connect with, so it's not the physical part that really counts. The soul connection is what really mattered; it was where the love came from! That connection has always been, and will always be there, and I truly believe we can and will have easy communication with those souls again, much sooner than we can comprehend in our human brains. Can we communicate with them while we are still in our physical bodies? I certainly think so; the trick is to get the human shortcomings out of the way, so we can really hear our hearts. Unlike in the past where the majority of the communication was through outside words, we now need to communicate through inside words, or the words in our hearts. We also need to remember, that once we lose our physical body, we can clearly see the pure love that exists in everyone. Then, without anything in the way, soul communication might actually be easier, if the recipient is on board, don't you think?

Any time, any place, any thought of the dearly departed IS a communication from them. Soul-to-soul, they're sending their love and want you to feel the comfort of divine love, in whatever way that moves you closer to it. Never allow our human shortcomings to block out that strong tie you have with someone that had to move on; honor yourself and your loved one with the faith that your connection is eternal and that you chose to be in each other's physical lives here out of divine love, hoping to help each other move closer to the truth that love is all that will ever matter. I'm sure it is our departed loved ones' wishes that we learn all we can about acknowledging each other's souls as much as possible before our time is through here, and that we follow our heart and continue our journey stronger than before, because of them. I'm sure that's all they wanted for us, that we learn to listen to our heart, always in what we do here, and also so that we can hear them as they continue to love and try to help us.

Next time you're missing someone that has "gone on ahead," remember, they're simply existing in a new place we can't understand, possibly right on top of you, patiently waiting until you wrap up everything that needs to be done in your current place. Communication is not impossible, just different than what you were used to; get all the gunk out of your life and out of your mind and let your heart speak, loud and clear. It's there you will feel that divine love of anyone you have a soul connection with. It's there you will find peace.

Sincerest Sympathy and Love to all with Grieving Hearts, *~Mary Anne*

THANK YOU FOR ALL THE TEARS

by Mary Anne

Thank you for all the tears,

saying you already miss me so.

I want you to know I didn't choose to leave you,

it was just my time to go.

Our hearts are connected in a way that never breaks,

so even if you feel broken now,

try to remember I am here,

closer to you than before.

I love you more than ever,

with a divine love unknown as a human,

and so I don't expect you to understand

until it is also your time to join me, someday.

Just know that time is not yet here

and you have much left to do;

using the love you learned from me,

the rest of your life here will always be true.

Always remember I live on in your heart

because I love you so;

I am always here to talk to,

more available than before.

I see, hear, and feel everything you do,

everything, and more.

That's all you have to know,

don't waste time trying to understand;

for one day you will know the answer and all will be clear.

And realize I chose for you to be in my life,

through good and bad, and all this strife;

together, we can get through this,

as impossible as that seems,

because nothing is more powerful than my love for you,

you helped me live my dreams!

Thank you for choosing to love me too,

that's truly all I needed,

to be ready to move on to my next world

with my heart as full as it could be here.

I know you miss me beyond what you feel you can take,

but keep me in your heart, listen and feel,

and I'll help heal that heartache.

When you think of me, please smile!

Know when you think you hear or feel me,

that it is me, being with you in the only way I can now.

That's why it's so important for you to listen to your heart

above all else, as we always should.

I can talk to you there and show you my love

and call in the Angels, God, and all help from above.

Believe in my love, with you through eternity;

the crying and pain will ease eventually.

I hope you can hear me and find your heart again;

there is a reason your time has not yet come.

Trust in my divine love for you and use your heart to love;

I was here to teach you that and it would honor me so,

to feel my time with you--past, present, and forever—

also made your heart grow.

MY TAKE ON JAMAICAN TIME

Awareness

November 2013

I dedicate this article to the exquisite hosts at Bromley, Alex and Johnathan, their wonderful friends and staff, especially Conney, and the dozen sparkling souls I spent a whole week with: Mickaela, Val, Robin, Vicki, Taylor, Kathleen, Paige, Emily, Steve, Cheryl, Mckensie, and DJ! Much love to all of you for teaching me so much!

Sorry, but I have to brag a little about taking time for myself (as I so often recommend to others) and jumping into a week-long Wellness Retreat in Jamaica that my good friend, Mickaela Summers created. I'm hoping this will become a regular thing for her and her good friend, Val Hickman, because it comes so naturally to them, and I've since committed to doing this for myself at least once a year. It was the best vacation I've taken so far in my life! I came back home rejuvenated, to say the least.

While there, we learned the term, **"Jamaican Time,"** explained to us that if someone says they're coming over or doing something later, it could be anything from a few minutes to three days, and no one has any anxiety over the exact time. Not by coincidence, some other widely-used phrases used there are, "No Problem," "No

Worries," and "Ya, Mon." Wouldn't it be awesome if these were the normal replies in the U.S. too? And wouldn't it be great if we could always operate on our own time, or at least most of the time? It's sad that we don't expect it and that we're often surprised when we get what we want, in this country, isn't it?

I came home promising myself I'd do my best to operate on Jamaican Time, as much as possible, but I've expanded the definition, based on my observations of the wonderful group of people I spent time with there. I'm going to call it, "Mary Anne Time" and I suggest you name your own time and methods after yourself, too. No matter what, you need to incorporate whatever your dream of "time" includes; it needs to be as individual and unique as you are. Only you know what it's best for you, no matter what!

That's the first point, to **spend the present moment doing whatever is fun and happy for you**, no matter what anyone else is doing, and no matter what anyone else expects of you, at the time. Now, obviously, we all have certain responsibilities, but even so, we can find lots of ways to keep our focus on something positive, such as focusing on the fun you can have with people or thinking about your dreams, rather than on mundane tasks. Truly, the majority of our time is ours, to choose what to do. Whether it's free time or chore time, usually we can still ask ourselves, "What do I really feel like doing, right now?" I always try to do this when looking at housework, since sometimes I'm just in the mood to do dishes rather than laundry, etc. As long as I'm doing something productive with my time, who cares what order it gets done in?

It's all about staying **TRUE TO YOURSELF**, at all times, or at least, as often as you can. It's about not being concerned with what anyone else is doing over what you want to do. This trip gave me every example possible, from sometimes wanting to cleanse and heal, to other times wanting to indulge and express every side of my being. Some times were for serious, deep, still meditation, while other times were meant to scream and yell or play and dance. Some times were meant to share, while other moments called us to keep our thoughts to ourselves or even spend some time alone. At times, we were inspired to teach one another, while other moments were for learning. Time was spent growing, along with time spent staying in our comfort zones. Nature called us sometimes, while touristy, socializing needed to be felt other times. Some moments were made to be warm and dry and basking in the sun, or taking on the protection of cloud cover, while other moments were made to swim in the rain. Many precious moments were spent flying and falling, with the next moments supporting or catching, literally! We all had both sad, heart-tugging moments, tears and all, and ecstatic, belly-filled laughter, often accompanied by tears as well!

For an entire week, I watched the majority choosing to honor themselves by doing whatever their hearts were calling them to do; the positive environment overwhelmed me to the point I have a new dream. My new dream is to live the second half of my life here, surrounded as often as possible by people that respect themselves enough to do whatever their hearts call them to do, without any regard to judgment by themselves or others. In my mind, this is the essence of unconditional love of self and others. Additional love comes in to play through the **automatic benefit to others when we follow our heart.** Trust it, try it, and pay attention to all the good that appears for everyone!

Throughout the entire trip, I savored being on "Mary Anne Time" wherever it called me to, moment-to-moment. It was incredible, and I had to scold myself a little for not learning this valuable, self-loving act sooner. Before this trip, I had slowly learned to give myself some time to choose whatever I wanted, here and there, but really only in recent years of realizing how important this is to my well-being, and to the rest of the world. Somehow, it just sank in deep on this trip, possibly from the whole group always encouraging one another to follow their heart and do whatever they wanted to. It's right in line with the Jamaican phrase, "Anyting you want!" How fitting! **All I have to do for myself, at every moment, is "Anyting I (my heart) wants."** In other words, do whatever makes your heart feel full and joyful, as it allows us to be the REAL person we are meant to be. This includes choosing to really be how we want to be, in all moments, rather than self-inflicting pain when we decide to be stressed. Stress is self-made; no excuses here. No one else can create it for you, even when you have something you need to do, or somewhere you need to be, even if you don't think you'll enjoy it. You still get to choose what you do with all of your moments! Why sabotage your precious moments?

I'll forever think of Jamaican Time as leaving the whole stress of what time or day it is, and the fear of what others think behind, as it really robs us from focusing on what we really want to be doing or thinking about, and it's the ultimate sin against ourselves. My cell phone didn't have any service, even to display the time, and it was such a blessing. No one minded ringing a bell for meals or when it was time to get up, or to tell me what time it was if I had to be ready to go play in the river or waterfall. Someone is always keeping track of time, so I really don't need to, all the time. I can't even tell you how relaxing and freeing it is, to not care. Just making yourself live moment to moment, choosing to do whatever you want honors your heart and your true essence. Please give it a whirl whenever you can, and **just enjoy BEING!** I also recommend saying this out loud, replacing my name with yours, of course, "I show myself love and respect; I'm on Mary Anne Time!"
Much Love, ~Mary Anne

WHEN IT JUST WON'T GO AWAY!

Difficult Situations  ***January 2014***

I think I can cover the whole gamut here, of major weights that drag us down, and seem to never go away:

- Frustrating or harmful relationships (often unbalanced because you give more than the other person)
- Self-defeating habits or ways of living (from the way you don't take care of any of the following: your mind, your body, or your spirit)
- Memories of things or people to the point it obstructs the present or your future
- Illnesses and any kind of physical problem, including extra weight
- Random, unfortunate events, bad luck, or people being anything but kind

Sometimes, it's just too much, and we feel like a sitting duck with our feet sealed in concrete with our hands tied behind our back, out on a major freeway, just waiting for anything that comes by to hit us! The human side of us will want to pretend there's nothing more than what we see on the surface going on, and it often persuades us to allow it to hammer on our self-love. **DON'T DO IT!** It will only prolong the process, I assure you from my own experiences! And if you do tend to feel this way, don't badger yourself for "failing!" We all have to learn, somehow; the key is to **LEARN, and LEARN FAST!**

I will tell you though, being human, I still spend time in these pits, but I'd like to think I recognize it a little sooner, all the time. As soon as I acknowledge what's going on, I remember that if I reconnect the dots of who I am, I can resolve anything. We are made up of more than just our mind alone, or just our body alone, or just our spirit alone. The three of them were made to work TOGETHER and **THAT'S WHERE YOUR POWER LIES!** Moreover, once you get that the three of them are connected during your time on earth, you start to remember that you are also connected to a higher power (God, in my book), forever; **CONNECTED ALL THE TIME**, no matter how much we choose to deny it, sometimes. **CONNECTING THE DOTS of who you are is the most self-loving, self-respectful, truthful thing you can do; therein lies all the answers to your pain!**

But our ego (or our demons, lies, disconnectedness, or warping from the outside world) would have us take a different route, out of habit. Our dark side prefers we honor it and rot forever, if it had its way. It urges us to strike back against others, life, and sadly, even ourselves. Ignore the spirit, it shouts! Destroy your body, it pleas! Give me control of your mind, it demands! **YOU ARE ALONE, it lies!** Its army consists of shame, guilt, regret, pain, anger, grudges, competition, or any of the lower energies that make us feel awful about ourselves and awful about life.

This army of harmful energies convinces you to feel helpless and alone, to pity yourself, to hold past memories in the present, to worry about and fear the future, to compromise your values in exchange for something, and to set yourself up for failure because of your fears, especially of change. Basically, you don't spend your day feeling the way you'd REALLY like to feel, instead you feel like you're at the mercy of anything that comes by next. **You've given up. . . on yourself, the worst betrayal of all.** : (It feels like SH**, doesn't it, even if you do it for only a moment or two? In my opinion, that's where all the crabby, mean, depressed, judgmental, self-destructive, and abusive people come from. They've given up, first and foremost, on themselves.

I know all this is giving you an icky feeling, and if it has, there's hope for you! **IT IS THAT AWFUL and IT IS HAPPENING ALL THE TIME, sometimes, TO YOU!** The faster you identify it as such, the faster you can change all of it, yes ALL OF IT! Remember, you only need to take care of yourself and the positive effect from that radiates out to everyone else, even if they don't acknowledge it, it still affects them in a good way! **So really, all you have to do is CHANGE THE WAY YOU LOOK AT THINGS, starting with KNOWING YOU ARE COMPLETELY CONNECTED, to all three parts of yourself, all the time, AND TO A CONSTANT LOVE OF A HIGHER POWER. ALWAYS! Use the power of this knowledge!**

Some quick tips that work for me:

Recognize when the Ego's Army has arrived and instead of letting them take over with the crappy feelings, realize there is **MORE TO IT** than what you are seeing through your murky lens!

Remember that **EVERYTHING, BUT EVERYTHING, HAPPENS FOR A GOOD REASON and AT THE PERFECT TIME.** There is a greater lesson for you to learn, a higher part of yourself to discover, or something bigger trying to come to you, in ways you could never, ever imagine!

Trust that **God knows what He is doing**, no matter how backwards it may seem at the time. Ask Him to help you understand the gifts you are receiving, as soon as you can comprehend.

Realize **you are a loving being**, and more capable than your human mind could ever fathom or allow. You were created in love and for love; you are here for higher purpose of yourself and others. It's far too much for us to understand in our physical form, but our spiritual side knows there is much more to all of this! Allow that thought to stay first and foremost in your mind, at all times, and you'll start seeing things you never saw before, no matter your age or life experience! Don't brush it off; don't let the ego convince you it's not real!

Believe that even when you think you're ready for something, like the start or end of a relationship or a major change in your life, you are not being denied it, if it doesn't happen according to your schedule. Most likely, all the pieces are not quite lined up out there just yet, to give you exactly what you've been asking for. It's not always just about you; sometimes you are there to help another learn something about themselves, but mostly, it's for both of you to learn. **To walk away without regrets, I personally need to feel like I did all I could in a way that was not self-destructive to me**. Honesty and love have power you wouldn't believe!

Almost always, God waits for me to realize I've been lacking in self-respect or self-love (again). (Man, is He patient!) I've tried everything there is, I think, from demanding others give me what I want, to just sending out loving, honest thoughts to others. Just guess which one works better and faster? Force is never the answer. **Love is always the strongest, for both you and everyone else.** Force may satisfy your ego temporarily, but love connects mind, body, and spirit and satisfies the heart, and that's permanent and it allows you to move forward! You know you're giving yourself love when your heart feels warm and full, and that's always the way to peace.

God did not put me on this planet alone, therefore**, I am not meant to always conquer my demons alone**. Personally, I pray for awareness of where God is guiding me (I ask Him to hit me aside the head with it, because sometimes, I'm a little slow!) I go back to things I've learned and I try to stay open to new perspectives and learn from others (good, bad, or unknown) and if my heart is drawn to a person's words or actions, I try to take the time to draw out what part of it was meant to help me. There is a benefit to me, in every single interaction and thought, but I know I miss it, most of the time. I have to keep reminding myself to stay alert in the present moment so that I can see it!

Sooner or later, if I just get back to recalling that I'm here to learn and grow, mostly in divine love for myself, God, and others, I start to see things clearly and I pick up the slack where I haven't been giving myself a chance to stay in the higher energies of love, joy, appreciation, peace, and everything that makes my heart glow. Almost always, I am released from the person or situation as it miraculously resolves itself. **The teacher (sometimes in the form of a situation) always appears when it can bring us something our heart desires, and can leave once we've mastered the lesson.** Do yourself a favor. Learn the lesson and let the struggle disintegrate. If it shows up again, you'll know what to do, just don't lose heart because it's just there to be a quick refresher you probably needed to grow your confidence. Treat it with love and never stop being amazed by the all-conquering power of love!
Remember to love YOU—ALL OF YOU!
~Mary Anne

THE DIVINE PLAN BEHIND CHAOS

Difficult Situations  ***April 2014***

As I lie in bed with the following words streaming into my head, I bask in the peace and comfort of it all. The understanding and beautiful sound of silence, complemented only by the reassuring hoots of the owl outside, every couple of minutes, seem to say, "There you go, you're finally listening!" Of course it's the middle of the night; when else do I allow myself to shut down the chatter in my head long enough to hear the words coming from my heart? As I finish the sentence before this one, I notice my new friend outside is quiet now too after about an hour or two of hooting, having delivered his message, urging me to get up and write.

I smile over all the chaos behind me, and how we always have the choice to allow it to drive us mad, or to jump on that crazy train and let it take us on the wild ride and rest stops we desperately need. What have I learned? Chaos is the Divine's way of taking over and telling us, "Hey Dummy! You are NOT taking care of yourself," or "You are NOT taking care of this situation," or "You are NOT on your rightful path," or the likes of these. It knocks us on our butts and insists we take a rest and re-think things a little while it shifts our life, right in front of our eyes. Most times, it's directly for us, but often too, it's because we are supposed to closely witness something that is meant to teach us and others something as well; usually, it's both, so pay attention!

Try to look at things this way, the next time it all hits the fan or never seems to end, or you're trying to find some meaning to something that seems very unreasonable or unfair; trust me, it'll help you an awful lot. Also, remember DD and DDD. You know DD as Designated Driver; remember, others under the influence of chaos may need someone to guide or drive them safely. Try to be there for others, it'll probably help you, too. DDD is **D**o it with **D**ignity and be **D**one with it! This is a reminder that it's good and healthy to let your emotions out! Let yourself be sad, angry, scared, and happy . . . whatever you need, but do your best to make it a place and time you are comfortable with. **DDD**, don't drag out the drama; it'll only drag out the chaos! You are allowed to be human, because you ARE human!

We never know quite when the perfect storm starts brewing. For me, this time had to be at least 3 months ago, as I tried to pack every life change I could into a short amount of time. My Honey and I took the big step of buying a place together, so I started the process of moving 3 kids and over 20-some years of stuff to 3 different homes. This included the adjustment of my single-Mom daughter and her son venturing out into the world on their own for the first time too, and me adjusting to letting all my little birds leave the nest without my hovering over them. Let's be honest, the big change can be very unsettling to all of us at times, so emotions really flare up. As a parent/grandparent, I'd just pray daily that they remembered how much I loved them and that if it was the best thing for them, I'd let them stay forever, but we all know better. I try to hang on to a little sanity by reading and listening to books I can learn something from. The right ones seem to end up right in front of me, all the time.

As I tried to downsize and get my home ready for sale, my Honey was too far away for us to help each other much, and doing the same with his previous home kept him occupied. I was on my own, which was nothing new. My day job also started demanding excessive attention and hours, so naturally, my health started to give out. I was still working on a swollen lymph node from the breast tumors I had gotten rid of, but started pushing it to the back burner, ignoring my tiredness and headaches that were starting, and decreased time spent exercising; there was too much to do. I just wanted to get things done and get settled in my new life, where things would be peaceful and time would be mine again.

Well, it didn't take long for life to tell me I had it all wrong. Monthly migraines started and demanded I pay attention to some other symptoms that always came with them; I knew I had to be off-balance with hormones or something. A quick visit to a new wellness doctor told me my nervous system was blocked and it was struggling at the level of a 70-some-year-old. That would explain why I felt that old, for sure, but I didn't stop to do too much more about it, really. I didn't research it like I should have. Then, I caught the flu one day, where it knocked me down hard enough to have to take a day off my day job, even though I work from home. Moving around much had my body temperature to the boiling point and about passing out, so I had to camp out in bed, thank God. I never get sick, ever, so this got my attention. It was time to do a couple of things I'd been putting off.

I realized at that point, I'd been ignoring the increasing swelling in my face and head and the pain, tiredness and muscle issues, and brain fog that accompanied them. Sure, I'd google the symptoms here and there, but didn't stop to pay attention much. I did go to the doctor the day before I got the flu, but didn't feel like the antibiotic they gave me for a possible deep-rooted sinus infection was doing much. It was also very odd the nurse didn't make a note when I told her I had slowly stopped taking a thyroid med because of the monthly symptoms I was having, and that they should check my blood. The doctor sees me so little, they usually do this every time I'm in there, but this time, I was home before it occurred to me they hadn't drawn my blood. I would have called and gone back, but I was also loaning my car to my son, whose car died, so he could get to school and work. Well, so today it was time to get on my health issues, among other little things on my "to-do" list. I had the time to sit in bed with my laptop and go after these things.

A pinched nerve in my neck or a flare-up of one of the neck bones I had broken years ago seemed like the likely suspect, but the monthly symptoms kept making me think of hormones. Either way, I wasn't sure what kind of expert out there could help me. I printed off more stuff to read on my upcoming vacation and vowed to try to get to the bottom of it while lying in the sun the following week, and I certainly did. Thankfully, I knew from past experience not to fight it when it started to resolve itself in its own way. I made myself get on the crazy train and tried my best not to take innocent bystanders with me, too much.

I felt better than I had in a long time after my flight south and even slept in, every day, knowing I needed the rest. It didn't matter. I had the strong desire to heal, and my body was demanding it now. The first day I had alone, I was forced to go to the ER, as the swelling was out of control and my body and brain started to shut down, for no reason I could find, whatsoever. Just as I hung up with the on-call nurse, my Mom happened to show up and have time to drive me there. Urgent Care was an option, so we tried that first, but quickly left when they told me they weren't equipped to do labs or to take my insurance. To the ER, it was. The Divine Plan had a female doctor treating me that happened to have a couple of thyroid diseases and she didn't hesitate to run a lot of blood tests and found me with the highest numbers she's ever seen. I had no choice but to go back on the thyroid replacement medicine I was certain was causing my other monthly issues, but I sat in that ER alone long enough to commit to several other things, including taking care of myself and getting the right experts to help me get to the source and onto another solution, as soon as possible. No more putting this off and just listening to the MD tell me to put a band-aid of a daily medicine on it; it just wasn't cutting it and my instincts told me, it was probably harming me more than anything. (So had the wellness doctor I had been to, just a couple of months prior.)

As I sat in the ER by myself (my choice) most of that day, I pondered some bigger things in life. I didn't mean to; they just kind of came up, at that point. My life was going through a major shift in purpose, like it or not. For one thing, I knew it was time for me to leave a big part of my old identity. It was time for me to step out of my role as always taking care of loved ones and onto something else, it seemed. The signs had been there, and God was helping me let go without guilt. They needed to take care of themselves, mostly, and that was quite clear. I knew I had taught them everything I could. Every one of them had expressed they couldn't take any more of my advice as well; it was all enough! (Can you imagine, with the passion we each have to cram everything we know into the heads of our loved ones, so they don't have to go through the rough lessons we've learned? I know it's just way too much, but I appreciate them loving me, all the same, as annoying as I know I have to be!)

So now what? Was it really over that fast? Did I have to stop being the nurturer and move on to helping the masses, just like that? I didn't know if I wanted to. . .

having to put loved ones first was always a good excuse to gradually work my way into saving the world, at my own pace. Was I ready for this, already? The thought was overwhelming. Was I wanting to do that, in this lifetime, or was this life's purpose over? Holy SH**! How did I get here so fast? Still, I couldn't deny the desire and all the preaching I've done on the topic; I know it is all our destinies to follow our hearts and allow our real selves out and that our real selves help save the world from itself. I was being called out now to dive in, head first. Holy SH**!

I had no complaints about the 5 hours I sat on that ER cot, just waiting for test results and re-testing results, barely visible to anyone, it seemed. I needed the time to absorb all of this, because my human instinct told me to tune it all out, and I certainly wasn't prepared to try to explain it to anyone. This was a journey I needed to start in on, on my own. I welcomed the time I was forced to sleep in and take extra naps the next couple of days; I was exhausted, but it was a good excuse to spend the time alone and in the quiet.

I realize this is a path I've been on, but it doesn't make it any less scary as I step onto it, for real and for good. It's funny though, how it makes the whole health thing secondary. However, I am more committed to taking care of myself and it is resolving itself, as things always will, once you get the main point of the lesson. The first day I was back from vacation, the exact right people expressed concern over my swollen appearance and dropped the right key words and leads that took me to the right experts within days to get to the bottom of all this soon. Sure, I had to tell my doctor that just staying on the med and checking back in a month was not acceptable; they just have no way of knowing how debilitating it is, at this point, I guess? I already know the specialists will help me figure it all out and resolve the source of the problem and I will have valuable information to share with a ton of people with similar health challenges. I've said it before, God bless the MDs for saving lives and treating symptoms fast, but it is not their responsibility (nor are they authorized) to treat our whole body, which is all tied together, remember . . . we need to take the care to do this for ourselves! I'm betting 80% of you women need to see the same specialists I am, an Endocrinologist to see what's going on with hormones and such, and an Integrative Medicine (whole body)/Alternative & Natural Hormone/Thyroid Expert. Both are covered by insurance, so I'll be posting on Facebook how things go and refer them, if I feel they are honest and thorough, trust me. My opinion is that all the environmental and toxic things have most of us dealing with crazy health issues because it is affecting our chemical balances, especially.

Oh, to see the light at the end of the long tunnel I've been turning around and around in for months, and to hope I have some shred of sanity left! I have gained some valuable life lessons in the process and life-changing meanings to life, so yes, it was well worth it and yes, I'd go through all of it again to get here. I admit though, I pray I don't have to because I'm not sure what miracles brought me and those close to me through it; I can't ignore that someone up there carried me most of the time, if not the entire time, (including enlisting help from earth angels that said or did the exact thing I needed, at the perfect time) and I am so incredibly grateful. Thank you, Chaos, thank you . . . and nothing personal, but I hope I continue to learn to listen to my heart more so you don't have to step in again and make adjustments. When you do, help me to quickly remember you are only here to help, and that fighting you only prolongs your visit. With gratitude for your patience, God, *~Mary Anne*

JUST LISTEN !

Awareness  *May 2014*

I keep hearing those words in my head lately, "Just listen." It makes me think about how much that applies, in every area of life. Just think about the value of listening to the following things. . .

Nature. No technical noise or interference, whatsoever, just nature. It's such a beautiful thing and such a rare thing to get, these days, unless you make a little effort. Any effort to make life better is such a good thing! Just sit outside for a few moments or go for a long walk, without any gadgets, and see how fast you find peace. Even the quiet has a noise, and it has the opposite effect on your body and soul than a phone making noise. Even when you hear other people or unnatural things, you quickly remember, you are in a big, full, busy world. There's so much going on you never notice!

To More Than Just Words. Words are often exchanged without thinking and without feeling. Most times, if you just pause and listen to the tone of voice, the meaning behind it, and sometimes, the sheer ridiculousness of it, you'll quickly realize that the words coming out are not REALLY what's behind it all. People are often distraught and overwhelmed, in zombie mode or about to explode, and so the release is done through the mouth to whomever happens to be nearby. Just let others vent sometimes; wait and watch their facial expression and really listen to the stress and plea for help in their voice. Most times, you will quickly realize the aggravation was not really fueled by you, at all. Usually, it's their nightmare of re-living hurt that was inflicted on them, often years ago! But, it doesn't matter a bit where their frustration came from; you only need to realize that you were the one that is strong enough to not take it personally. When people lack strength to deal with things, they reach out to others to help with the weight of their world. You off-load some of that weight from them when you just take the time to look at the bigger picture, and don't attack back. Remember, when SH** is tossed your way, just side-step it as respectfully as you can, instead of letting it land on you or throwing it back.

To Your Body. A series of ridiculous, crazy, and unforeseen health issues in the last year or so reminds me to honor myself by trusting my instincts more and listening to my body right away, not "when I have time." We get so busy and put off our health all too often. We can think it's going to go away, but it doesn't. It only tells you something when you need to listen and help it out, so don't take it for granted. Ignoring it is disrespectful to yourself and that will always come back to haunt you. Sure, we don't always know what it needs, but we do need to drop things more often and figure it out, right away, instead of putting it off until it knocks you down in the form of an injury, permanent health issue, failed body function, or life-threatening disease. There are so many ways to research and get help these days, it's incredible that we still try to douse the signals when we get them.

To Guidance, in Every Form. Tracking down the causes of my health issues has been quite an adventure. Sure, you have doctors and experts and healers of every kind to go to, but there are also suggestions or comments from family, friends, strangers, articles, and endless other places to get help. It has been a large combination of all of these, plus inspiration or something I randomly caught on TV or radio, that is helping me track down the long path of overcoming my health issues. The first thing I realized I needed to do was trust that God would lead me to it, and to be patient as He did. Second, I needed to focus on the lessons or purpose behind what I was going through. For me, it was a couple of small things about taking care of myself in every way, getting more practice listening for the clues and intuition, and big focus on what I want in my future. I have made an incredible amount of progress in all areas because of the health setbacks! Never judge or second-guess. Follow what is put in front of you, no matter how odd it may seem. That takes me on to the next thing we all need to pay more attention to. . .

To Whatever and Whoever is With or Around You at the Moment! No matter how odd, unexpected, or uncomfortable, you are always exactly where you are supposed to be to give and receive something. Can you learn something about yourself, others, life, or another step to get what you want? So many times, we tune out to our immediate environment with electronic devices or escape through addictions or habits and miss it completely! Then what? Well, I would imagine that life has to try to show you whatever it is another way, another time, which only delays something you are supposed to have or know! If we ignore long enough, I personally feel life eventually shakes us up and sets us down on our butt, in an attempt to make us see or face whatever it is. Trust me, that's the hard way, so why not cooperate with life? It's only trying to help us!

To Your Heart. This requires the most commitment of all, to trust and respect what that gentle, little, kind voice inside is telling you, about anything. "Rest. Go talk to that person. Look around you now. Know you are exactly where you're supposed to be to learn to love yourself more. Be kind to yourself. Be kind to others. Let your curiosity guide you to the next step. Believe the world is on your side." The beauty of this is, because your heart is always with you, you can do this anytime, anyplace. If you let the busy world take you over all day long, at least take the time whenever you're lying down…before you fall asleep and just as you wake up are powerful times to listen and focus on only what you want. That small practice alone, done with a good, self-responsible attitude, can change your life! Believe there is so much beyond what your senses can discover, and that's where your heart steps in; it knows. We only have to LISTEN. You won't believe what you've been missing! *~Mary Anne*

TO THINE OWN SELF, BE TRUE

Self-Love  ***June 2014***

Who's in charge of your life? You think you are? For many of you, I call BULLSH**! Chances are, you are NOT in control of your life . . . you are just SO fooled into thinking you are!

WAKE UP! (Please?) If you don't read the rest of the article, I've already proven it to you. **That THING that's controlling you already told you not to read the rest of this.** It gave you some bullsh** excuse that you shouldn't or don't need to or don't have time or whatever. If you are going to read the rest of this, good for you! There is hope for you and for your life. You are one of the strong that could survive! (Yay!!!)

So if you can handle it, ask yourself, what am I doing with this life? Am I wasting precious hours, precious days, maybe even my ENTIRE PRECIOUS LIFE? What AM I DOING?! Oh, don't stop thinking! Please don't stop thinking! Don't fade off into zombie mode so fast. (Boy, is that "the way to be" these days!) LET the REAL YOU come out, at least for a couple of minutes, to finish reading this. Give your life a chance! You were created to LIVE and to do SOMETHING with your life. Why else do you think you are here?!

The zombie/the ego/the dark side/our demons rule over most of us, most of the time. The more we feed it, by giving in with habits and excuses and truly, just lack of plain old thinking, the more control it has. But it's NEVER too late; if you think for a moment it is, well, that's just your dark side lying to you again. It's what it does, you know . . . lies. Keeps most people fooled until they're staring in the face of death and realizing all of it with overwhelming regret. Is that where you're planning to be, when it's your time? Must be, if you still don't take the time to turn on your brain. You're just a walking, talking, dummy suit. You're not real.

See, the REAL YOU, if it were in control, would not harm itself. The REAL YOU would take precious care of everything about you and your life, wouldn't it? The REAL YOU wouldn't push away all or most of the really great and good things in life, would it? WHO'S IN CHARGE OF YOUR LIFE? LOOK IN THE MIRROR! It's okay, don't be afraid! That "thing" ruling you will tell you not to listen to me and it will probably even tell you to get so angry about this, that you never listen to me again; it has to protect its kingdom, somehow. Obviously, it will scream at you to PUSH AWAY anything that honors your real self because its only mission is to stay in control and destroy your life. Did that register with you? **I'll say it again, "ITS ONLY MISSION IS TO STAY IN CONTROL AND <u>DESTROY YOUR LIFE</u>!"**

Still don't want to believe this is you? Okay, but I warn you, your REAL SELF is going to have to take over for a minute and allow your brain, your heart, and the honesty of your soul TURN ON. See, if they're ON, light and truth shines on all the BULLSH** and you will see everything clearly. It's that easy. Here's some simple ways to tell who's in control of your life:

→ Do you push away opportunities for the good things life has to offer you?
→ Do you stuff your face with toxins, junk food and drinks, and maybe even overeat and drink, like a pig?
→ Do you zone out or avoid thinking things through, constantly distracting yourself instead?
→ Do you think and talk about other people or events more than you do your own life?
→ Do you think other people and random life experiences are to blame for who you are and where you are?
→ Do you surround yourself with people that do all of the above so that you don't feel guilty?
→ Do you avoid people or things that ask you to THINK?!

It's really very, very simple. In anything you're doing, you just have to ask yourself, "Does this honor and respect my mind, body, and soul, or does it betray even one of them?" WHY would ANYONE IN CONTROL OF THEMSELVES HARM THEMSELVES IN ANY WAY—the body and its health and longevity, the mind in allowing it to think things through, or the soul in living an unlimited life, filled with dreams and bliss? If you were truly in control, you would not inflict harm on yourself, would you? If you were truly in control, you'll pick up this article and read it again, and again, and again, until you pull back all of the power you have given to that side of you that wants to destroy you and waste your entire life. **If you were truly in control, you'd see the light and the simple truth and take back the rule today . . . NOW!**

And don't be fooled. No matter how long you've surrendered your life, you can regain control very quickly and very easily . . . just turn on the brain to start and think things through. **Ask yourself if what you're about to do REALLY makes sense to you? Is it HELPING your life? If it's not, you are literally ROTTING AWAY, even before you hit your grave. It's always one or the other, helping or harming.**

There you have it! If you're helping your life or honoring and respecting any part of you, YOU are in control. If you are NOT helping your life, you are betraying and disrespecting yourself and your dark side is running amuck. Simple. Sending love with big hopes you take back control because EVERYONE LOVES REAL PEOPLE, and frankly, ZOMBIES SUCK, in every way. *~Mary Anne*

THE GARDEN OF LIFE

Awareness  ***July 2014***

Many of you know I have a new home I haven't moved into yet, as I'm working on selling my old one. I eagerly planted a nice-sized garden at the new place, thinking my boyfriend would tend to it a little between my weekly visits. After all, he had helped get it ready and even planted some seeds, so I assumed we were in it together. The weather and my brief visits kept me from the garden, and I asked and reminded my boyfriend to help me out with watering and weeding, but all he did was water it a little. By the time I could spend some time in it, the garden was nothing but a thick bed of weeds, many to the point of seeding out.

Human nature had me furious inside over all the precious time, money, and energy wasted, along with my boyfriend's disregard for something that he knew was important to me. But that only lasted a moment, as I remembered that by now in my life, I had a habit of just trying to love people no matter what, and that everything that challenges that desire is meant to teach me something more and to help me grow into the better person I am destined to be. So, while I could accept that I didn't like it, I still knew I had to keep loving him (no, I choose to keep loving him), even as he took a nap while I spent hours slaving in the mosquito-infested weed bed.

I put on my "conquer the world" attitude and went in. The hours of carefully and painfully (I have carpal tunnel in my dominant hand) trying to remove the weeds and hope for something I planted underneath to show itself gave me lots of quiet time to think about what this was trying to teach me, and it didn't take long to come to me. This garden was like life, plain as day.

First, I couldn't blame anyone for not nurturing or sheltering my garden (my life) from anything. I had planted it, I wanted it, and I was the only one responsible for it. While most people would have given up on it (as they do on things and people in life), I refused. I wanted to find something better underneath. Some call that naïve, some call it crazy or unrealistic, but I call it desire, and I felt very wise and loving about it. And forgiving my boyfriend for the incredible mess I had to deal with now honestly felt pretty good too; just knowing I was capable and didn't consider whether he deserved it or not felt pretty good. (Even afterwards when my entire body was sore for days, and I had the worst sunburn of my life across the back of my waist!) Am I getting back at him a little, telling the world all this? Yea, I kinda hope so. . . ;)

Second, it became very clear to me how events and people in my life compared to the things in my garden, so much so, that I felt some emotions as I worked.

The handful of weeds I was throwing out were the big messes and people we need to leave behind in life, because our heart tells us, it is not helping us. Boy, is there a LOT of that! At times, I feel that's ALL there is, and it'd be easy to give up all hope that there's nothing good left. But I can't believe that, or I'd become a weed myself and then really, have no reason to continue on this journey. So faith and trust keeps me going, and eventually, I would find something good underneath. Sometimes it'd be a long time and what I found looked almost non-existent, but there was something there, and finding it felt like finding treasure. Not because of what I found, but because I hadn't given up; it didn't even matter if the plant I found would survive or not. All that mattered was that I had come for it. There were times too, I was surprised to uncover a strong, healthy plant, or even a nice row of them; they had not been visible at all, to the rest of the world. It was pretty cool to finally see something no one else could!

Other times, I'd notice that I had pulled out a good plant, along with the weeds, and I'd feel bad, like I was rushing too much or was being too careless. Then I realized, I was doing the best I could, and maybe it was just not meant to stay there and grow. This could be compared to people that leave our lives for any reason. I know by this point in my life that once they have finished the lesson they are meant to help you with, it's just time for them to go, for various reasons of their own life. It truly wasn't my fault or my doing; it was just meant to be. Sometimes they choose to leave and sometimes their dedication to something or someone else forces them to go (like great friends I had lost because they had to "pick a side" with someone or something else they felt they needed to stick with, for whatever reason.) It was all okay; we would all be fine and continue our journeys.

Sometimes in trying to do a good thing by pulling the weeds, I'd bump a stem or a branch of a good plant and hurt it. Sometimes this happens in life, though none of us really intend to hurt anyone or anything in our life. We just have to do the best we can, apologize and nurture what we can going forward, perhaps through some extra attention or effort. It also told me to slow down a little and look more closely before proceeding, a good lesson for all of us, all of the time!

I didn't finish the garden that day. It will be a work in progress, like life. I'm happy to say I'm well over half-way though, again, like my life, as I approach 50, and at least I caught most of the weeds that were trying to spread bad seed on my garden. Most days, that's a very good day in life, isn't it? After all my effort, I am happy to report that there were a lot more good plants down there than I expected. Yes, the neglect choked out and killed or stunted a lot of the good seed I had planted, and that's too bad, but again, my focus only needs to be on what's left now and what I can do with it. How do I know? Maybe the soil just wasn't the right kind for those plants? There's no point in continuing to look for, or be upset over, what didn't happen; it's gone. The fragile plants that are left need my care and attention now. This is a great reminder to live in the present and do our best with each moment we are given, and NEVER look back on the past, except to remind you to live the present to the fullest.

Certain things in my garden (I guess what was meant to be, despite what I planted originally) will thrive and I will reap the benefits of it. I will also continue to work on the weed patch that is left, and whatever shows up later; it's just what we do in life. There's also room now, if I want to plant more seeds. There's nothing stopping me from trying again. Maybe it just wasn't the right time before, and it's never too late. The beauty of it is, with the right attitude and effort, we can live in a beautiful garden, every day, and never give up when a few (or a lot of) weeds show up. The weeds will teach us something, for sure, if we just keep our heart open to it, so it's always good, just like everything truly is, in life. Tend to and enjoy your garden, and ask God to bless and watch over it. . . it's the only one you got!
~Mary Anne

SOME PEOPLE WILL NEVER GET IT!

Difficult Situations  ***August 2014***

Some people…you could kick them in the head and they will still never get it! They drive you crazy, pushing you to the limit of your anger, sadness, energy, and headaches. Some break your heart and you are baffled at how they can have any conscious at all. Don't they ever just stop and think about what they're doing? You pray that maybe, just maybe someday, they'll get it, before it's too late. I always want to give people the benefit of the doubt and I hope people do the same for me, but take my advice, don't bet on it and don't hold your breath in the meantime!

What's WRONG with these people? Surely, they must know what they're doing and feel some remorse? Again, don't assume, and don't expect them to act any differently in the future. Even if you've repeated your wishes to them a million times, in every shape and form you could imagine. Even if you've tried to say nothing, hoping the effects of what they did would teach them. Even if you've dropped hints, or even got to the point of being very direct with them, sometimes exploding or crying or begging . . . don't expect change. Oh, you can hope (and I usually do, even if I won't admit it), but don't be too upset if miracles don't happen, be it overnight, or over a lifetime.

Before I go on, I have to clarify. There are two distinct classes of people in this frustrating category. The first is obvious after a while; you are supposed to part ways or at least distance yourself from them because there is no mutual benefit to continuing your interaction with that person or perhaps that group of people. Once you respect yourself enough to do this, people more suited to you and your mission in this life can start to show up in your life, and everyone is happier. The second group may torment you for life! These are the people that are either related to you, work with you in a job you love, or that you choose to commit to for life. Oh, you'll feel like you should "be committed" some days alright! Now, let me emphasize that just because someone's in this second class, it doesn't mean you are stuck with them. There's always a way to distance yourself emotionally or even to cut ties completely, if that's what's meant to be. No matter what, your obligation is to take care of how things affect you and to strive for positive experiences as much as possible. You are always in control, no matter what anyone else does.

That said, your job it NOT to control what others do, but to control what YOU do. No matter what anyone else does or doesn't do, YOU still get to decide how you're going to let it impact you, if at all. I've had enough of these unpleasant experiences and frustrating people in my life to now understand a little of the bigger picture:

That person or that experience is trying to HELP ME in some way, and when I look at the situation from that angle, I don't get so upset or stay upset so long. After all, being upset is such a shameful waste of your precious time and energy! I truly believe that every interaction is trying to guide us into something better for us, and it's usually pretty personal. Maybe we need to learn to be more independent and to pursue our desires and caring for ourselves a little more. Maybe we need to learn to practice standing our ground without offending anyone else. Maybe the people you sacrifice everything for really don't appreciate it or grow from it, and it's time to start following your own dreams, and stop doing so much for them. (This is a BIG one for parents…I believe we stunt the growth and ruin a child when we do too much for them, especially when they made the choice to risk a bad situation they now want our help with; don't do too much or they will never learn, and never learn how to take care of themselves the way they should!)

Life is about evolving, and maybe some of the things you'd settle for before, or even do before, isn't helping you or your life anymore. These things can be very obvious, if you just open your eyes and your heart, but if you miss them, something upsetting will happen to try to get your attention on it. Often, we don't know it's time to move on or to look at something else, or that the person frustrating you has bigger issues than you'll ever understand. And so, I sincerely believe that God puts these people in our lives to nudge us towards something we are supposed to do or learn. We may not see it right away and sometimes, not at all, but if we keep our hearts open to the possibility that whatever is going on must have a greater positive good behind it somewhere, it's much easier to handle.

If you feel like you're hitting a brick wall as you try to work with this person, maybe it's the wrong way. Maybe you need to turn around and find another way, which may include being true to yourself, whatever that may bring. No matter how your loving actions are perceived by the offender, as long as you act with self-respect and genuine care for that person's highest good, everyone wins! Doing what's best for you, in a self-loving way (which means handling things with as much dignity and compassion as possible) will always have a good impact on others, no matter what. Again, you may not see the benefit, but it'll be there, even just to make the person stop and think that if you won't put up with it, maybe others will give them a hard time with that behavior, too. A person that respects themselves will always be respected by others, deep down, and it will always provide the chance of teaching others to respect themselves and others. It's always good.

Now don't get me wrong . . . some people will make wonderful changes in their lives, all because of you, and we can all deal with that. Don't give up on them, as long as it doesn't harm you, including holding you back in any way. Just try to remember, some people will never get it, and maybe they're not supposed to. Perhaps a big part of the reason they're here is to challenge us until the day we die, so that we are learning and growing, until the day we die? Also, I would imagine there are some people we've encountered that feel the same way about us . . . maybe we are also among those that others feel "will never get it!" Maybe we drive some people crazy too, because we're here to help them learn something more about themselves? It's a crazy-beautiful design, once again, and all we can do is trust, some days. There's always a gift in it somewhere, some way, someday, even when we can't see the gift in it all. Just trust. *~Mary Anne*

EVEN GOD RESTED

Self-Love  ***October 2014***

I've been in high gear for as long as I can remember, even as a kid. With hard-working, driven parents, they knew the value of every single one of us, and so, we all helped with everything, from a very young age. Best thing my parents could have ever done for me. I hope all of you parents are paying attention; it's never too early to teach your kids anything, especially their worth through some simple chores or letting them help you.

And so, I was used to always being busy. It is probably part of my identity. We got up early, long before we were even in our teens—as early as 4 or 4:30am, sometimes—to make sure things were taken care of. Sure, I complained about it back then, especially on a well-below-zero winter morning when it was still dark out, and we had to go outside to take care of the cows. The gigantic barn that must've taken every ounce of credit my parents could get to build was still cold, cold enough to make your hands hurt while we spent a good 3 hours milking cows. We worked hard, but I realized before long, my parents worked even harder, and for what? To make sure we all had a good life . . . all 11 of us kids. That's love.

Being raised with it makes it easier when you get older and have to make your own life, I think. I couldn't believe how easy working for someone else was, and how much they were willing to pay me! But I was more floored by all the complaining everyone else did about working. Really? I was just grateful to not have to do such hard physical work anymore and to have part of the day, or even full days off, on the weekends! My natural habit of being busy kept me busy for years, even when I wasn't working. If I wasn't helping someone with something, I was raising a family or volunteering somewhere. Then when my kids got old enough to be off on their own, I found other things to do, to try to help people on a larger scale. I feel blessed to have that in my blood.

Once I got older and wise enough to realize there truly wasn't ANYTHING stopping me from doing ANYTHING (why does it take us so long to learn this basic truth that we are born with?), idea after idea poured into my head. Books, articles, workshops, and ways to help myself and others evolve into more of their real self gushed from all sides. Even in using the middle of the night, I couldn't keep up with making notes on all the wonderful ideas I had. My personal life took off, too. Before I knew what hit me, my youngest was out of school and my boyfriend and I were living in the home of our dreams, a location with a lot of land that gave me a ton of new ideas. Abundance was flooding us, and that's all I ever asked for . . . abundance in love, life, energy, happiness, etc. You name it! It was all so . . . overwhelming?!

My busy life got the emergency brakes pulled, hard enough to spin me around and make me wonder what direction I was facing? My health gave out, despite most of the stress in my life was happy stress. It started out slow, as if to warn me, but I didn't have time to slow down or pay attention; I just kept moving forward. There was so much to do to sell our homes without warning, help my kids all move out and get settled, enjoy the new grandson, move everything to the new home, and keep going with my RISE ABOVE work, including the new books and projects related to it, and really start my NEW LIFE! It was all so exciting, but I was missing it.

I didn't want to complain about wanting things to slow down, because I was living a dream that only got better and better, but deep down, time was slipping away without me understanding where it was going. I tried desperately to find more time and energy to enjoy things, but it only exhausted me. My body gave out.

My old self would've gotten depressed or angry about the unfortunate timing, but the new, wiser me knew there was a very good reason and that somehow, it was for my own good. I looked hard for the answer, hoping to figure out what the reason was, so I could jump back on the fast track, but it didn't come for months! I spent about a half of a year just trying to find enough energy to get through a normal day and not need 12 hours of sleep plus a couple of naps during the day to keep from passing out. I spent about another half of a year recovering. What was the turning point? When I finally accepted the fact that the reason for this craziness was probably nothing more than to make me STOP.

I was living in paradise, but I didn't have time to look around and enjoy it! I was starting my new life with my boyfriend, but we were both so exhausted at night, we barely spent any quality time together. I hadn't had time to just sit and catch up with family and friends in months. That's no way to live. People are the reason we live, but I wasn't getting to the people! I kept working hard, thinking I'd get to the end of the busy days, but it didn't come. As I was forced to just sit still (literally, as I was too weak to move because my body was deteriorating fast), I started to realize that my wanting to do it all was too much, and God didn't want me to have to do all this. God wants all of us to be deep-down happy, and I think He was just trying to hit me aside the head again to remind me what I REALLY wanted.

My boyfriend and I were not taking the time for each other, period. In my mind, relationships either grow or die; there is no ***nothing*** when living things are involved, especially people. People are the most important thing there is. Everything else is just here to help us, so letting the busy stuff get in front of our enjoying our time together wasn't the way it was designed. Making me stop long enough to see this was invaluable. So, being too sick to go out and do things socially gave us a little more time for just us. Nothin' hurt. My relationships with my good friends continue to grow, whether I see them often or not; we all just appreciate and make good use of the times we do get together. Random people care more than we ever know, stopping to ask how you're doing and sending up prayers without our knowing.

I know there are a lot of other reasons for this "slow-down period" in my life, like getting to the bottom of some life-long health issues, helping some people close to me be more independent and appreciate me more, making me more aware of what is best for me, and making me do some of those things I'd been putting off, setting up the perfect release times for my next books and projects, and many other things I may never have a clue about. I've been through enough now to know I just need to trust that God is trying hard to help me have what I ask for: **"Whatever is for my highest good."** I'm not afraid to make this simple request anymore, because I know God loves us more than we can ever comprehend and all that is for our own good will never leave us sad, lonely, unfulfilled, or holding the short stick. We always win, and so does everyone else, if we just trust and look deep, deep enough to see the truth. So, I'd like to send you love and the awareness to clear out any SH** that fools you into thinking otherwise; I am thankful that comes back to me as well!

So I'm going to focus on taking it easy and looking around and enjoying all that life brings, for now, because it's okay to rest, sometimes; we know that even God rested on the Seventh Day! *~Mary Anne*

WHEN TO CALL IT QUITS!

Difficult Situations  ***November 2014***

I've seen enough in my day to be a firm believer that there's a divine goodness in everything. In other words, there's a reason for everything. I believe this is especially true in the really hard things in life. When you get to the point of feeling like you just can't take it anymore, I say it's okay to call it quits.

While there are endless possible reasons for our pain, I think one of the biggest reasons for the pain is to try to force something to change. I think we all can agree that without some uncomfortable things that have occurred in our life, we would never have gotten to where we are. Not only can it shift your whole life around, but it moves other things and people around as well. But the biggest thing it does is change YOU, with or without your permission! If you can be honest with yourself, I know you realize that something in your past that you didn't like deserves the credit for something wonderful you discovered in yourself. You GREW because of it, or you shifted your life, or the people in your life, in some way. You know this!

Hang on to this reality when you are frustrated with the biggest challenges in your life. What IF it's just trying to help you CHANGE your thinking, your

direction, or help you in some way? I know how harmful worry and stress are, so I use the following prayer a lot:

"Okay, God. I don't know what to do and I'm not sure I can get through this. I don't understand this, but I trust you. I know you know what you're doing and that you love me and want me to be happy, more than I could ever understand. Carry me, help me to get through this and if it benefits me, please help me to see the good in all of this, as soon as I am ready. Thank you, God."

Most of the time, once I accept what's going on and give up trying to control it, I start to see things I didn't before. As my perspective broadens, relief seems to start appearing, like magic. Something new comes in, kind of like when a woman gives birth. Fighting the pain and the natural process that must occur only makes it more difficult, but once accepted and working with the process, it seems the new life can finally emerge, and instantly, most of the pain is gone. Sure, there may be some additional healing that continues, but you hardly notice it, in the joy of the new life; it was all worth it! It's the same way with any struggle in life.

So "just surrender," or "give it to God," or "let it go," but do we really get what that means? To me, it's very simple. If something's not working, look for another way; another option, another path, another perspective. GIVE UP what is not working! Sometimes this means giving up trying to figure it out or to just trust it's going somewhere good. Sometimes, this means letting go of people, or letting go of the *type* of relationship you wanted to have with them. The truth is, you were born alone and you'll die alone, so there is no one person that you would die without. It's just you and your Maker, really, when you get to the very bottom of it all. Other people are necessary to help us learn, yes, but when the learning is over and all that the relationship brings is harm (versus help) it's time to let it go, at least to the dynamics of the relationship you had in mind.

Once you really release whatever is burdening you, the new, wonderful thing can start to emerge. Sometimes it comes in slow, at the pace *you need*, but don't be surprised if mountains seem to move overnight! Even in people or situations that you were hitting a brick wall with, they change so drastically that you can't explain it. And when it doesn't change, it's your blinking sign to move on! Maybe it's completely, or partially, but you'll know what you need to do. Whatever's good for your heart and soul is always what's good for others too, especially in the case where you're enabling someone's lack of growth because you just kept putting up with it.

No matter who they are, or how afraid you are of losing them forever, follow in your heart what you know is best; LET GO, so that something new has a chance to come in. Don't waste your time analyzing or trying to control it, just continue to let it go and heal yourself, and appreciate the whole reason for original struggle. **TRUST!** Apply this to everything, from issues with the body, the mind (and emotions), and the soul/spirit. It all works the same. Death or destruction allows life or new growth and rebuilding, stronger than before. Out with the old, in with the new, because sometimes, both cannot occupy the same space!

Let me give you an example from my life. 2013 and 2014 were the years of big health struggles for me. Looking back, I'm not surprised, since I sped through several major life changes, on all levels. I had a little bit of everything going on and no one doctor could figure it out, so I just kept looking for answers online and seeking out other doctors, especially the natural healing doctors. What held me back was not going INSIDE myself enough to embrace my emotions and work on healing those, even though I'm a firm believer that we heal from the inside, in this way. Maybe I wasn't ready and maybe the time that passed had to, for some reason, but as I allowed myself to look at how I felt about everything in my life, the perfect healers started to drop in my lap.

First to come were those that could help me release and heal my emotions; that big stuff took me months and months, as I am still human. But then, once I got to the end of my rope on the things I couldn't work through, I decided to just let go of a couple of relationships and beliefs, finally realizing maybe that was what was best for me, despite how much I thought life wouldn't be worth much without them. Grieving, I was just honest with each person, and let something with them go, telling them I had tried everything.

Then, BAM! A friend called to tell me about an almost-free opportunity to see a few spiritual healers, and I let her schedule me with all of them. I was floating on air when I left those sessions and not coincidentally, those relationships I had let go changed for the better too! I also had new hope that I'd get to the bottom of the lingering health issues I still had, with nothing but tests showing hints of a Lyme's Disease band and some autoimmune stuff that was stumping the MDs. Next, I walked into a Health Fair one day, that happened to be across the street from a meeting I had later that day and BAM! A wonderful Eastern-Medicine Professional told me I had Lyme's Disease and that he could easily cure it and my allergies, etc. as well. We all assume helpful people like this are going to take all our money, but I went to him and I can assure you, he does it all for almost nothing! I got a fast education from the Eastern-Medicine Pro that Lyme's Disease is VERY common, VERY contagious, and often behind many other health issues, and my entire family could have it. He brought this up and recommended everyone be treated at the same time to avoid re-infection.

Just like that, my boyfriend with the massive joint aches, my son with the stabbing pain in his abdomen that the MDs couldn't figure out, and I went to get our allergies and possible Lyme's Disease cured. And BAM! For almost no cost, we all walked out of there with not only cures for the Lyme's Disease and multiple food allergies we all had, but bonus healings on organs, foot pain, my thyroid, and simple things we can do to STAY healthy in the future. I should mention that just days before, thanks to a new friend of mine, I ended up at a "Healing the Thyroid Naturally" presentation where that Naturopathic Medicine Expert assured us that with the proper nutrition, even my thyroid could re-learn to function on its own, despite the 40 years of neglect and abuse. This has been my dream, and when this Eastern-Medicine Pro echoed what I had just learned a few days ago, I was elated! And to think, all I had to do was release my struggles . . .

So don't be so attached to your old ways or your old life. We are meant to grow and learn our entire life, right up to our last breath (and probably beyond, but we'll just focus on this life!) If we're not, we're dying, aren't we? And so, we will suffer a slow death as long as we fight it. Me, I'm not into pain, and so I try to stay open and aware and embrace it, saying, "Okay, I know there's something good in all of this; what do I need to know, learn, or do differently to get to the good stuff here?" There's so much to learn! And while I don't always remember this, my desire to remember it usually brings something about to remind me of this very simple design, and for that, I am so grateful.

The other big thing to remember, is that suffering is not necessary for us to learn. I just need to make more time to take care of myself and my life, in all aspects of mind, body, and soul, and allow myself to learn the easy way. That way, life doesn't have to present the challenges to force me to learn what I'm missing, or if it does challenge me, that I don't struggle as much, but instead, simply allow myself to learn! God help me learn the easy way! *~Mary Anne*

HAVE A REASON TO NOT LIKE THE HOLIDAYS?

Letting Go  ***December 2014***

Do some, or even ALL holidays bring you sad or hurtful memories? CONGRATULATIONS! You're in the club! The "I have good reason not to like holidays" club, that is. Oh, and you're not alone; in fact, this club is far bigger than the "Holidays have always been wonderful for me" club. So what are your qualifications? Please mark all that apply:

- ☐ I wish my parents had done, or would do, things differently
- ☐ Someone I love, or loved, let me down or hurt me
- ☐ I have no one to love and feel forgotten, like no one cares
- ☐ I miss someone terribly, or I feel lonely, even with people that love me
- ☐ I'm too tired, sick, busy, broke, or broken-down to care
- ☐ Other people or things ruin it for me

I'm gonna wager that you meet more than one qualification and that more than once, felt like life was a little unfair to you, giving everyone else your share of happy. Sometimes your share seemed to go those that really didn't deserve or appreciate it! It's no wonder you don't want to enjoy certain or all holidays; the fact is, you don't feel like there's anything *to celebrate*!

Again, you're not alone. Even if this doesn't describe you, I can assure you, you don't have to look too far to find people that feel this way. They are EVERY-WHERE. While certain heart-breaking memories seem to have been created on or near a holiday, I'm thinking the whole thought of stopping to celebrate reasons to love and be loved, like holidays and special days, just emphasizes everything. And who wants the absence of love emphasized? Not this girl! Yep, I'm part of the club, too. I'm just as human as anyone else. Boy, could we have a giant pity party together, I'm thinking!

But . . . hang on. Even on days that are not holidays, those memories still exist, don't they? They are written in our hearts, and though no two hearts are exactly the same, we can understand each other's pain, as we have felt it too. **Pain is pain, and heartbreak is heartbreak**; it all hurts a great deal, no matter who you are or what caused it. Chances are, all of us have fallen into that awful pit of despair, hopeless about ever finding a way out. Some days, those dark walls surround us again, out of nowhere; it doesn't seem to matter how long ago it was, or how far you've come since. Once it's etched in your heart, you don't just forget. I say, that's okay.

It's okay to know where you came from. It's okay to prove to yourself you could survive. It's okay to have another day to decide where you go from here. It's okay to realize that YOU and the world live on, for very good reasons. It's okay to know that YOU are the only thing you need to rely on, because no matter what, YOU are never alone. The whole time, there was a higher power with you, mysteriously carrying (or dragging) you through when you couldn't take it anymore. To me, it's God, and I know He's always part of me, no matter how low I feel, and all I have to do is acknowledge there is light somewhere (acknowledge Him), and somehow, I get through. *I'm still here.* I MADE it through! Think you can't do it? But you ARE doing it!

Sad memories are just that. They are MEMORIES of your PAST. Today, though, is NOT the past and wasn't the pain intense enough the first time around? Chances are, you've re-lived it now, too many times to count. You are proof that what doesn't kill you absolutely made you stronger, and you know it. You survived because you were DESTINED to. You have today, now, for a very good reason, but today can't come to you completely if part of you is still stuck in the past! How do you get out of the past, though? Simple. Add something to today to make it DIFFERENT and BETTER than the past, regardless of your current state!

Sad? Do something that makes you happy. Lonely? Do something for others or with others that makes you feel good about yourself. Think you need someone to make you happy? Take the time to just be by yourself, appreciating who you are, or letting yourself experience something new. (By the way, it's okay if your "by yourself" time is around other people.) Missing someone special? Write them a letter to thank them for what they taught you about yourself or about life. The letter is just for you, to do with it whatever will help you remember to live a new day EVERY DAY, and to live it BETTER because of your past. Stay focused on good memories and lessons that you can use to make today and beyond benefit from what you've been through!

Remember that no matter how sick, broke, tired, or stressed out you are, you are constantly choosing to love or deny yourself, too. Where's the benefit in inflicting additional pain to yourself? Apply good ideas you get to any situation, and let's continue. No family traditions you want to carry on with your family, or no longer can? Start some new traditions. Some people I know do wonderful things, like construct a garland/flower holder over a loved one's tombstone and decorate it on special days. Most believe they can hear and see us, so if it makes us feel better, why not? You are free to do whatever you like, you know! Required family gatherings not so fun? You're still the boss of you, and thus, your level of fun too. It may help to remember most others have pain in their past, and not everyone can find their way out of it, and just function in whatever way they can. Be kind. Find your fun, somewhere, even if you have to go hide out with the kids. They make their fun!

Honestly, it's not for me or you to judge. The only person I truly need to be concerned with is me, and I remind myself that my actions *matter*. I know that what helps me automatically helps others. What hurts me automatically hurts others, because no matter how alone we may feel, the truth is, we are NEVER alone. Someone, somewhere IS connected to you, or IS SUPPOSED TO BE connected to you. When you don't allow your true, peaceful self to live this life in a way that is joyful to you, you deprive EVERYONE ELSE that is destined to be connected to, and enjoy life with you, and often, BECAUSE OF YOU! You matter so much more than you know, so don't keep yourself from the world. That's my greatest wish . . . try to help me out. Much love to you! *~Mary Anne*

WHAT'S WITH ALL THIS PAIN & SUFFERING?

Difficult Situations  ***January 2015***

I'm sorry, I just have to say it out loud. What the he** is going on? Shouldn't we be EVOLVING as a world, not deteriorating? Yes, I am an Optimist, but we can't argue with the stats that more people are getting sick and dying, more world struggles are occurring and yes, the whole planet is slowly dying! I'm not paranoid; I know I'll be just fine, no matter what, but lately, it's all I can do to watch people struggle, usually unnecessarily, in my mind. So let me take you into my mind, for a few minutes, if you like . . .

All our man-made medicines and apparatuses are NOT healing us, for the most part. Hey, technology and science is great, but people just aren't taking the time to THINK for themselves, in my opinion. If they did, they would KNOW some things just don't add up. Like if all the money and resources we're pouring into our overwhelming health issues was effective, WHY do we know so many really sick people and people taken from us by a common illness? Now, don't get upset, thinking I'm referring to ALL modern medicine; some is wonderful and safe, but you have to admit, the majority does more harm than good, if you get ALL the facts from an unbiased source. That requires you look at everything, from all sources, and do your OWN THINKING!

Apply it to anything in your day. Is what you're eating safe? Are the gadgets and appliances you're using safe? REALLY? How so? Because the person getting money for them says so? (This includes the government—they get a cut too, remember.) WHY ON EARTH would someone admit that there's a risk it could kill you? They know that would discourage you from spending money on it! Sure, there are some with a conscious out there, but they pretty much have to walk away from the selling side or desensitize themselves, altogether.

And let's talk about desensitizing, for a minute. Most think they have to not have any sensitivity or conscious or even, any brain of their own to "fit in" to this world. They don't want to be different or have others not like them. So what do most people do? They lock up their heart tight, most of the time, and tell it to be silent! Why? Because the heart & soul KNOWS when something's not right for you. Not healthy, not ethical, not logical, not part of the TRUE YOU. Seriously, what a sad world we live in, when we don't let ourselves be our TRUE SELF! It's the ENTIRE REASON WE WERE BORN, and we literally waste our life, when we don't let our real self out!

This is the UNNECESSARY stuff that just kills me. Someone will fill you in on a struggle they're having, like a health issue. They've been to the doctor, maybe many times, but no healing is evident and they're getting to the point they are worried they will always be sick or that they could even possibly die from it. Yet, they continue to look for answers in the same way, usually by going to the usual medical doctors. Does that make sense? If you took your smartphone back to the same place over and over again, just to have it not work, over and over again, wouldn't you maybe look at another phone or even another dealer, eventually? WHY don't we do THAT with our health? Moreover, would we just let our smartphone sit in a drawer at home and never use it again (let it die slowly and NOT replace it)? WHY do we do this with our body, then? No, we can't replace our body, but we CAN replace what we're using in and on and with our body! We CAN go to a different kind of healer or modality or thinking for healing! What's stopping us?

Oh, we don't want to be different or we don't want to change. Maybe deep down, we don't believe we are capable or deserving or maybe we think suffering is GOOD? Again, does this make ANY sense to you? So what is my magical, wonderful solution? STOP! THINK! LET YOUR HEART OUT, FOR GOD'S SAKE! Re-learn to listen to it! IT HAS THE ANSWERS AND IT KNOWS!

How? It's so easy! Take a moment to THINK whether an honest, deep thought you have is making your heart hurt or feel cold or scared or doubtful, or ANYTHING negative. That's telling you it is NOT TRUE FOR YOU. It is telling you, that's NOT THE RIGHT WAY! Now, if you feel just the opposite, like warm, growing, loving, full, happy, excited, hopeful, strong, or ANYTHING positive, it's the joyful message that it IS your true self and a path you are destined to follow! Let's take an example, now.

So many people I love do very little or nothing about a health issue. They seem to enjoy the pain, attention, or conversational matter it brings. You hear every excuse, from, it's just age, or it's hereditary, or my doctor said I'll just have to live with it, or no one knows how to fix it. There's even worse excuses, like old beliefs that haunt people to convince them suffering is deserved or required for forgiveness, or good because it means less suffering later, or that one person's suffering means less for others or advancement to something better? Or, "It's just how it is!" Am I the only one that feels ill just thinking of how crazy this kind of thinking is? You can't tell me that any of this thinking makes the thinker's heart GLOW?! I know it makes them feel bleak and hopeless and alone. I KNOW they are NOT remembering to listen to their heart!

I KNOW GOD is an all-loving God that truly doesn't want ANYONE to suffer. He loves us completely, even though He knows exactly what we're thinking and doing. He ALWAYS forgives us and wants us to do the same. He created us in and of DIVINE LOVE; anything else is our illusion or the result of our free will, including the choice to continue suffering instead of changing a thought or action of taking care of ourselves. NOW, sometimes suffering IS intentional, as a way to learn and get through to another milestone in our life, or to help us to forgive ourselves and make up for something we feel we need to in order to forgive ourselves, but I think we truly can reach that place without suffering too, if we proactively worked on it. See, everything we do (or sit back and don't do) either helps or harms us . . . there is no "nothing" or "neutral." And then that radiates out to everything and everyone around us, so even if we don't feel WE deserve to be healthy, we should still strive for health of mind, body, and soul because whatever we are pours out onto everyone else.

That's the facts, in my mind, people, because that's what makes my heart feel strong and warm and true. I encourage everyone to un-learn thinking solely with their head and moving it back to the most powerful, truthful part of our being, our heart, and just see the miracles and HEALING that occurs. I am a little passionate about trying to help myself and others remember this, after going through the vicious cycle for almost a two-year run, myself. In fact, there are great things brewing on my horizon because of it, and I'm so excited I can hardly wait! My heart wants to take off running after it, which is an incredible feeling you just have to try out. You'll rarely slip back to not wanting to do your own thinking, ever again! *~Mary Anne*

IT'S OVER. NOW WHAT?

Change  ***February 2015***

It finally hits you. IT'S OVER. IT'S REALLY OVER! Natural human emotions go wild, dragging you through sadness, anger, confusion, self-doubt, heartache, and general feelings of failure or deep loss. However, if you're willing to allow yourself to see beyond that tiny, tiny focal point, you may get some positive, random emotions thrown in too, like relief, excitement, forgiveness, appreciation, and a general reflection of some valuable learning experiences you went through. You're still in control of what you let yourself see and feel; you're always in control, even in this gray, cloudy place.

I'm convinced there's really no such thing as "endings" in life, only BEGINNINGS. We all accept that two things are inevitable in life, as we know it: Birth and Death. I say, our entire life, including that part when we're in human form, is just a series of births and deaths; something has to end for you to go to a new beginning. People have written about this forever! Something has to be destroyed to be rebuilt, you have to be burned to ashes in order for the phoenix to rise, the caterpillar must let go of its current form to become a beautiful butterfly, and on and on. The point is, you can't arrive as your new self or on your new level by staying in your current state. You have to release or let go of something to GROW or MOVE FORWARD in life.

Why grow? Why not just stay with your dream man or woman, or in your dream job, or in your dream home, your current state of who you think you are, or wherever you're comfortable and content? As long as your soul is getting what it wants and needs, you can. Your heart and soul will tell you, somehow though, if it's feeling stunted and confined, and I hate to be the one to tell you, if the heart/soul ain't happy, nobody's happy! It'll tell you any which way it can, until you or someone around you, starts to listen. Maybe things will start to sour beyond the point of ever finding sweetness again. Maybe your health will start to give out. Maybe something major and unexpected happens, to try to give you time to stop and think, or to see things from a new angle. Maybe there is a huge loss or betrayal or anything that makes you feel a deep crevice in your heart. Maybe you just feel like there has to be something MORE.

Usually, these things happen to me because I'm missing something big. Usually, I'm not learning something about myself that it's time to learn (and we never know when we are ready for that new lesson) or I'm repeating a self-defeating habit, which is always detrimental to others, by the way. Usually, I think I'm being a loving, giving person when I'm actually stunting another person's growth because I'm doing too much for them or enabling a behavior that it's time for them to grow out of. I try to remind myself that when it's not good for me, it's not good for others, either. True paths always line up to be mutually nurturing and beneficial to all involved, whether all can recognize it at the time, or not. Many times, we will never know. Just trust.

And when it's not good for both, it's just the end of that journey together. Change—and growth—is needed. Something HAS to end for the new to BEGIN. It could be very subtle, like a close, daily friendship evolving into an occasional communication or a small job promotion, or getting rid of something on the list of junk food, or it could be life-changing, like recognizing you and the person of your dreams came to a fork in the road and you no longer want to take the same road. This comes in a countless number of ways, from losing something you used to do together, ending a romantic relationship, or even in death. We have to realize, it's NEVER just because someone WANTS to LEAVE you and make you unhappy, it's ALWAYS BECAUSE SOMETHING NEW HAS TO START!

Even in death, most of us believe that we leave here to go on to something amazing and good, beyond our comprehension. Who's to say the deceased didn't have to go because it was just their soul's schedule—it was nothing personal, their time here was just up! If you were connected to the deceased, I'm certain we rejoin them once we're ready to go, too, and I really do think they often grow their love for us to the point that now they're ready to help us in a much bigger way, and that they can do that, once they're no longer in their physical body. It's not so far-reaching, is it? Love is much bigger than we can ever understand.

But WHY do we have to grow? Why can't we just stay where we're comfortable? Again, as long as that comfortable is allowing you to learn more about the true person you are (a perfect-just-the-way-you-are, loving person, here to help the world in some way), you shouldn't change anything about it. It's when we're not growing that we start to die. Every living thing in this world, including us, is here simply to grow, right? I believe we were born to grow, in some way. After all, our soul is the only thing that existed before our body and this life, and our soul is the only thing that leaves this life, right? SO, it seems quite logical (and heart-warming) to me, that the whole reason we're here is to grow our souls, which happens when we learn more about who we really are. I believe EVERYTHING that happens in our life is all to help us with this mission. EVERYTHING. So even the things we believe to be tragic or mistakes or bad luck serve a bigger purpose. If we only open our eyes a little more to see this bigger possibility, we can often find it, even if it isn't immediate. Again, the knowledge comes when we're ready, and all too often, we don't see it because we have a thick cloud of emotions or beliefs or fears blocking our view. It could take a lifetime to clear away all the clouds!

Trust. Let go of anything (feelings, beliefs, doubts or fears, people, routines, etc.) that is no longer for your highest good of loving yourself unconditionally and accepting who you are—a critical part of this world and here for a reason—and allow GROWTH (aka, more love and light) to arrive. When you do, you automatically do it for all those around you, whether they ever realize it or not, so it's ALWAYS a good thing and ALWAYS the right thing to do. Keep your eyes and heart open; there's always something wonderful there! *~Mary Anne*

DNA: IT'S DEEPER THAN YOU THINK

Awareness  *March 2015*

So right away, we all go to those things we think we're doomed with, when we think of DNA. Specifically, we talk about physical issues or genes we're just stuck with. It's just how it is, we think. NOT SO, says I, and while we're on the topic, let's talk about the other pieces of DNA we're always ignoring, shall we?

We tend to give attention to our physical self-our body-and ignore the larger, more important parts of ourselves. Our physical self really is just a tiny, tiny percentage of our whole self. Do yourself a favor and start to honor the rest of your being . . . you know, your mind and your soul? And you know how I'm always saying that when you do what's best for you, it's always what's best for others too? It works the same way, when you do something good for your body; it helps your mind and soul too! Likewise, when you follow the longings of your heart/soul, it becomes easier to take good care of your body and mind. It's all connected; it's all part of you and there's no way to deny it, despite how much you may sometimes ignore this basic truth.

That said, what makes you think DNA is only physical? If we automatically inherit our parents' bodily DNA, why wouldn't we also get the DNA of their mind and soul too, or in other words, their spiritual DNA? Oh yes, it's true. We are the off-spring of our parents, and their parents, and so on, in every part of our being—mind, body, and soul. Oh, feel the doom again! Did your little negative self jump right to what you feel is wrong with your parents, or their parents, or start to freak out as you think about your crazy relatives? Okay, chill out already, and stick with me. I think it'll be worth it, in the end! On to the good news . . .

DNA, along with everything else about you, is always, always in your control. Always! Your physical, emotional, and spiritual DNA still has to obey your free will. No matter what your inheritance is, the effect it has on you is still dictated by you. I realize this is not what you may have heard your whole life; the whole world often seems to give us the horribly-incorrect message that your genetics are something that have to ruin your life. Ya, ya, just like all the other excuses most of us have, of the things that "ruined" our life!

I have to gently remind you that no one but you can truly ruin your life. You still get to decide what to do with everything in your life, including DNA. Scientifically, you can see the effects that thoughts have on DNA. Chemically, biologically, energetically, and beyond, we have common tools to measure cells actually changing, based on thoughts! This is not new; this is not a break-through. Countless scientists and experts have written and taught with proof of all of this, not only in humans, but in all living things and beyond, even in the structure of water! Do you understand the power you hold? Do you see how your "faults" or "blocks" (as you may call them) may not be yours at all, but possibly something you inherited?

Afraid for your offspring now, knowing how you feel about yourself and your life? Don't be! Please! Be relieved, knowing you have the power to heal anything, once and for all, thereby healing it in not only your descendants, but I also believe it heals your ancestors too, whether they're still in the body you knew or not. Is this blowing your mind yet? It should be, if you're paying attention at all! Not only do you have the power to heal your life in all aspects of your being, but also all of your loved ones, including those that have passed on! This would take countless hours to explain in detail, even in my simple understanding of it, but I assure you, many have written the proof of all of this, so you can look them up, if you desire.

To bring this wonderful, loving, healing power into your life, once again, it's so, so simple! Do what's best for you. Heal your life, every part of your mind, body, and soul, and it automatically spills over onto everyone around you, especially your family, born or unborn, alive or deceased. It all benefits all souls, no matter where they may be. This knowledge overwhelms me and empowers me to listen to my instincts when it comes to the health of my being—mind, body, and soul. I rarely hesitate to allow myself assistance from the experts anymore; or from anyone, for that matter. In any form, the teacher/lesson will arrive when the student is ready! I've seen the incredible effect it has had in my life and in those around me. It also helps me understand the challenges that we all have with our standard behavior, habits, and beliefs. If you pay attention, you can easily see the patterns shared in blood relatives. It's not just the environment they grew up in, it's their DNA! And until a person decides to take action to change that DNA, it will continue to be handed down to the next generation.

We are sometimes devastated by challenges we face and wonder why we can't get past emotional, behavioral, or physical things we'd like to heal. It's sometimes not so easy when it's generations deep! "Why can't I get past this, or why do I keep doing this when I know better?" We ask this frustrating question, but we need to realize that sometimes, it's in our blood! Don't worry that you're broken and don't overanalyze why you are that way or look from someone to blame, just decide you don't want to be that way and that you're going allow yourself to change it or heal it or let it go! My secret when I can't quite convince myself that I'm capable of it, is to remember how powerful it is to resolve things with myself, as it will radiate out to my descendants, my ancestors, and anyone else around me, FOREVER!

Remembering it's not always your stuff makes it a little easier for me to remember that I'm not really so bad, after all. Neither are other people. They inherited everything they have, too! We've got to try to remember that everyone has a soul and are doing the best they can for their state of mind, body, and soul. No soul truly sets out to harm or offend another soul, so don't take things so personally. Their DNA could be to blame!

Just do your best to be the one wise and loving enough to alter the pattern and change the future. There is a good reason you are aware of this and you can make your path whatever you desire, both despite your DNA and because of your DNA! There is a reason you are seeing it all! Bless you AND your DNA! *~Mary Anne*

GOODBYE TO LIFE, AS I KNOW IT

Change  ***May 2015***

I'll be the first to tell you, I was terrified for months, to leave the security and comfort of the life I've been yearning for my whole life, but my knowing it has to be this way and the excitement for the adventures ahead is finally taking over. The rumblings, discord, pain and frustration of people treating me like I don't matter or don't fit in, and that I need to be something else to be important to them is finally enough. I finally realize that I'm finally allowing my heart to move from the almost constant pain in silence, into freedom. How did this happen? Life was looking good, on paper, yet I knew something wasn't right. The heart always knows, and unless you put a lot of effort into ignoring and numbing your feelings (which a lot of people do, their whole life, sadly), it's gonna get through to you, eventually.

I tend to make excuses for the way some people have treated me. "You're too nice," my good friends tell me. "You need to make people accountable for their actions and their life, or you're enabling them." I know this, all too well, as I still struggle some days with that gray area between trying to be kind and understanding or downright enabling someone, which only causes severe harm to all. I don't see it right away, because my ego feels good "helping" people (stems from one of my insecurities, sometimes), but I'm catching myself more and more because I realize that our role is to EMPOWER each other, not ENABLE. The only person that can truly help someone is THEMSELVES; each and every body needs to realize they are capable, period.

It starts at a very young age, when we teach our babies to hold their own bottle, then to dress themselves, and later, to earn their own money and successes and to move out and be independent. If we're not teaching our children these basics, we need to take a hard, sometimes painful look at ourselves and be honest about what insecurities in one's self is deciding to directly harm another by NOT teaching them what they can do.

I had to face this a ton, over the last couple of years. Life started moving forward so fast, I couldn't keep up. Sprinkle in some health challenges and relationship judgment days, and I had all I could take, some days, more than I could take, most days! I was forced to fall into survival mode, knowing I had to change some big things in my life. But even more was needed at this intense level; it was time to say goodbye to life as I know it and start a whole new phase of my life. How fitting, as I'll be turning 50 in a few months, and welcome in the second half of my life. Oh, I hung on with everything I had, but our deepest desires are so much stronger than we know. My mind didn't know it, as I worked like a fiend to put all the pieces of my dream life in place, but my heart knew. My mind is just now starting to comprehend why I've felt so tormented and alone, over the last two years, which should have been the happiest time of my life. I was fighting all of the truth from surfacing, but it always will, and it takes much more energy to try to suppress it. I ran out of fight, thankfully.

I'm hoping I've learned now to allow the truth always, for me. Perhaps the old way of thinking was kind of okay for those first 50 years, as I was constantly taking care of someone, and not just my kids. But I see now how enabling others made things so much harder for all of us. Then, once I realized it and pulled away pampering others at my expense, it was not well-received. People even hated me for it, so I highly recommend not enabling anyone to start with! Most will make you disappear in their mind, which is okay, since they were probably just an anchor anyway, taking something from you they shouldn't have, instead of facing their own self-doubts. Even though it's hard and they may never want to understand, doing what's best for you will always be what's best for them too. In the long run, you are helping them along in life, and you know it. Isn't that the most loving thing to do, really, no matter how they feel about you afterwards?

So what did this do for me? I had to let go, of most everything. The dreams I had and things I thought were important to me, were important at one point, but just no longer are. I achieved the dreams and they taught me something more about myself, others, and life, so they fulfilled their purpose and helped me grow. As I grow, so do others around me. Of course, others can choose not to grow—it is their right—and then, they just don't understand and they can choose if they want to be in your life anymore. I get to choose too, because sometimes others' not dealing with their own resistance to growth harms me, and I have to honor myself and walk away. It's nothing personal, no matter how close you were; it's just life and individual choices.

It may hurt very badly, but I've realized it's just the normal grieving process we need to say goodbye with, when someone or something, dies from our life. Just like when someone crosses over, reflecting on the appreciation and gratitude for what I've learned from them always helps. Nothing is a mistake; we always learn if we just allow it! Truly, it is always there to help us. I worked so hard my first 50 years to have everything now that I thought I ever wanted. I don't even know how I got through the last 2 years alive, honestly. It's been chaotic, but so have a lot of growth points in my life. But forcing me to the point of survival pushed honesty right into my face, and required me to pull it out of those closest to me, too.

The result? Most are taking off and flying, just now being forced to see they have wings too. As they do, they inspire and support me, beyond my comprehension . . . it's magical! Still, some refuse to even look at their potential and have already made me disappear. I guess I wasn't as important as I thought I was to them, after all! Sure, it hurts sometimes, but I still need to respect their choices. Only they are accountable for their own happiness, after all. My pampering or enabling them some more won't bring anything but harm. I am grateful they were some of my best teachers; I'll never forget what I learned about myself, because of them. Also, maybe we never truly felt comfortable around each other because I just wasn't supposed to be there, or it was forcing them to look at themselves? Either way, it's clear I was supposed to move on and not stay there.

So do you see how doing what's best for yourself will always be what's best for others? As I say goodbye, I have infinite opportunities. I'm overwhelmed, to say the least. I know I can truly go anywhere, do anything, and be with whomever I want. No more excuses, I'm FREE to be ME! On to the second half of my life—it's all brand new, FOR REAL! Prayers are appreciated; I have no idea where I'm going on this adventure of my new life! *~Mary Anne*

COBWEBS EVERYWHERE!

Change  ***August 2015***

Cobwebs everywhere, including in my brain! I had to take notice. I moved into some unused rooms by a lake that the spiders had become quite fond of, and it's in my daily routine to clear away the new cobwebs forming where I had just knocked them down the day before. (I'm pausing to kill a spider crawling on the wall next to me now . . . they are everywhere!) I don't blame them, they're in a prime location and they catch a lot of bugs and I appreciate that, but I finally came to terms that this is MY space now, and they have to go. So while I appreciate their industrious work ethic, I keep sweeping their work away from my living space and just outside my door, to keep the webs out of my hair, literally.

I'm like those spiders, sometimes, going through the same motions every day, even though what I'm doing is futile, because it's in the wrong place or at the wrong time, and it just doesn't matter the next day what I did. What a lot of effort for something that can't support me the next day! As I step into this uncharted time of my life, it's fitting that new acquaintances refer to me as "Mary Anne from Gilligan's Island" because honestly, sometimes I feel stranded on that unchartered desert isle with just a few others around me. I just don't know what's out there, or even what's here, right where I am and yet, I appreciate the beauty and the leisure of my new life; I'm definitely on an adventure, and a big one! I just have to learn to navigate a little differently now. It's all so shockingly new!

I know I've reached that point in my life where I just don't want any more of the stuff that creates those cobwebs in my mind or in my life. I want clear, clean, open space to move through to get to wherever it is I'm trying to get to; I don't want to be constantly spinning around to brush all the gunk and extra junk off around me. It consumes too much time, energy, frustration, and frankly, it distracts me from what I'd rather be doing; it traps me like the bugs that get caught in those spider webs! So thank you, busy spiders, for the perfect analogy to remind me of this as I destroy your works of art every day. It's just time for you to spin elsewhere, as I'm claiming THIS space now; I have better things to do than to clean up after you or be concerned with what you are doing or where you are choosing to go. The rest of the world is free to do what it wants, but I choose to do my own thing, in MY space, that is rightfully mine because I exist on this planet, too.

As I pay a little more attention as I'm cleaning up a web, I often spot the cobweb creator in the space we can't both occupy and unfortunately, I have to squash it, just like the beliefs, feelings, situations, people, and random thoughts that no longer help me be the person I know I can be. Let me be clear that I'm NOT recommending you fight anything; instead, face it, embrace it, and get to your true feelings. Be honest about how it makes you feel and why, and deal with THAT and choose to let it go. (I'll maybe write more on that process soon, as I've been working hard on this!) I send them off with gratitude for the work they have done here, but tell them they are no longer needed or wanted. That open space is for me to create my new dreams and truths about my life now, and I will take every bit of that space back.

Moreover, Mary Anne doesn't need to be stranded on her desert isle and sit in the middle of the tossed-upside-down life and unpacked boxes that seem to be following me. There's a gorgeous big body of water just beyond those cobwebs calling out to me every day, to come join in the fun; more wonder awaits! Again, fitting that such a huge cleansing mechanism is right outside my door, literally for me, just beyond the things that cloud my vision! Oh, for weeks, I was too damn busy to even dip my toes in the water . . . can you believe that? I simply admired the shine of the sun and the moon rays off the water from my bed for just a couple of minutes before I zonked out from exhaustion every night, and on my walk to my computer in the morning. Eventually I had to harshly examine myself and ask if I was wasting life? Again I reminded myself, we make no mistakes, just lessons and things we need to go through to get to where we need to be, so it's ALL okay! Time to do what I want more now, though!

So I'm continuing to work on getting my "sea legs" in my new life but I acknowledge, it's a good life, and soon to be great, as I ease into it. I'm letting myself do little

things, like take a walk before I start work and enjoy the amazing scenery and opportunities around me, and get out on my floaty once in a while. I bought myself a paddle to help me feel a little more secure venturing out away from shore a little, again reminding myself I need to allow myself this in life, too! Slowly, I'm working my way up to letting the wind and the waves gently float me around wherever I'm supposed to go; they are my friends and work hard to turn me in the direction my heart wants to go. Trust reminds me, it is my friend as well. By the way, I honor the new people in my life that tease me and keep me grounded by calling my little floaty, "The S.S. Minnow!" (Take that, you smart butts! Hee hee!) Allow yourself this kind of thinking, whenever you can . . . join me . . . the water's fine!
~Mary Anne

RESENTMENT: WHAT'LL IT GET YA?

Letting Go ***September 2015***

So life's been pretty amazing as I make a new commitment to myself for my next 50 years to take better care of myself, not just physically, but in mind and soul/heart too! I KNOW by now, that when I do this, I automatically take better care of others, too, and that benefits the world, instead of harming it, which tends to happen when I'm NOT true to myself!

Part of all this is learning to love myself a little more all the time, including those parts of me I used to not like, and so, healing (or at least steps towards healing) have to come about. It's nothing you have to force; it'll naturally happen on its own to follow the desires of your heart. So we all have those people that wronged us in our lives. Some of us could make a hell of a list and justify each one of them to make a soap opera series! The reality is, we all have our own little soap opera going on, somewhere. Don't be fooled into thinking only you were targeted for this bullsh**; everybody's got it! Those that don't show it have just come to realize it doesn't get them anywhere sharing it or dwelling on it.

We KNOW the truth: Holding on to anger and resentment (or any of the really negative emotions) hurts us more than the person you're angry at. Honestly, the person you feel owes you something could probably care less; you think they would have done it in the first place, if they cared that much? Even when they are aware of your grudge, do you REALLY think they care? Really, they don't, so what's the point in continuing to inflict self-harm because of something THEY did to you? You don't need them in your life to hurt you anymore because you're hurting yourself just fine, without them!

I KNOW it's hard to let things go, trust me! I recently had a run-in with the person I hope is the biggest challenge of this life, because it's about killing me. Seriously, I've been told for years that my liver is stressed, and guess what? All the experts say that the liver is where we hold anger and resentment! I've eliminated every other physical stressor of the liver, to my knowledge, yet that poor thing continues to work overtime. I very often feel it ache a little, as I do now, as I'm writing this! (Maybe it's cheering me on, to release this dirty, icky, sticky resentment for this person, as I write!?) At this point in my life, I DO believe that sometimes, and maybe all times, physical ailments are often the heart/soul's way of trying to get our attention on something or to shift our lives back to what we're really here to learn. For me, I tend to heal quicker when I take the time to acknowledge how I'm feeling about things and take some steps to honor and respect what I want out of life. It's worth a try, if you've got any aches or pains or issues going on!

Anyway, whenever I'm reminded of someone that was crappy to me, I know it's in my best interest to find the lesson that was there for me, appreciate that they were the teacher, acknowledge they were doing the best they could dealing with their own lack of self-respect/self-love, and MOVE ON! I've learned that suppressing it or ignoring it, like it never happened doesn't really do it. For me, I need to appreciate the interaction for what I learned, kind of observing the scenario as it replays in my head, instead of holding on to the "poor me, the victim" attitude. I have found that if I DON'T acknowledge the good in it, a similar situation comes up in a new place in my life to take another shot at trying to help me learn what I need to learn. I have to re-live the hell, all over again, sometimes many, many times! ARGH!!!

So this time, it was obvious that I needed to learn AND ENFORCE a couple of things. First, I needed to stop enabling this person by picking up the phone when they call; I had NO obligation to this person anymore, so why did I think I had to answer? No, from now on, I will always let those calls go. If there's an emergency, they can leave a message and I'll decide if I need to call them back, when I want to call them back. Second, even though this person was significant in my life for a very good part of my life and we have connections through other people, it was time to realize the relationship does not need to be in my life anymore. I don't need to be punished for the rest of my life because I was in a relationship with this person. I don't need to punish myself for making a "mistake in judge of character." I realized soon after everything exploded that no interaction is ever a mistake! Everything that happens in our life is to try to help us, in some way. We ALL do the best we can; there truly are no mistakes and certainly, while we can apologize when we hurt others, there's no benefit in punishing ourselves or suffering long-term because of it! I don't know about you, but as long as I'm human, I'm bound to behave in ways I'm not proud of, sometimes. Learning to be sincere with an apology is good for me too, once in a while, so I remember how to be compassionate and understanding to others; we all need it at different points in our lives!

Third, I was reminded that we are not all the same! Not everyone's priorities in life are the same as mine, but I still need to respect everyone else's life journeys. Only God knows why they are so adamant about putting other things first that I feel are low priority, but I do know something more. If we didn't have these people and events tripping us up and making us stop to take notice, how could we ever work through learning to accept people that are different from us, and respecting them as a fellow human being? How would our ability to LOVE ever evolve? We all know, it's easy to love someone that loves us for who we are, but what about those that don't? Can we find a way to love them too? (Deep down, we all know there is bliss in loving and accepting everyone; we just don't know if it's humanly possible, do we?)

So I've learned a couple of new things, reinforced some things, and I'm sure I learned more than I realize, but I was happy about some big things that came out of it. I didn't get lost in my anger this time, and allow it to ruin my night in progress with people I love dearly. I KNEW THEY were what I needed to focus on, not the ridiculous phone call I chose to let interrupt our fun! I apologized to them a couple of times, until they begged me to let it go. I love them for reminding me I had the choice to just LET IT GO! If it came to mind again the next couple of days, I needed to look at how it could HELP me and what else I needed to learn. Here it is, 5 days later, and I'm still learning and trying to put it to good use, but it's better than holding on to it for the rest of my life! I know, I DON'T NEED TO HOLD ON TO ANY "ICK" IN MY PAST!

So is it over, just like that? Well, honestly, my liver aching a little bit right now tells me there's still a little ways to go, but I'll keep working on learning how to heal from this. Naturally, this person's junk isn't the only thing in there, but I found it easier to work through letting smaller things go, especially from people I haven't seen in years. Little by little, I say a prayer or send out some love and appreciation to them for what I learned from them and wish them well. It just feels like the right thing to do, and I know to listen to what makes my heart feel good for guidance. It's the only way to go.

There must be a reason I feel the urge to go public with this today, so I'm guessing some of you will lovingly send me some feedback to help me continue addressing my sore liver problems. It's amazing how one little new idea can expose the doorway that's been out of view, so I appreciate all input from any of you. Not only is my liver tired of dealing with this one, but the rest of me is, too. Much love to everyone; take good care of your livers now too! *~Mary Anne*

WHAT DO YOU WANT TO BE WHEN YOU GROW UP?

Awareness  ***October 2015***

My Godson recently asked me to play with him and his siblings, in a make-believe game he called Business Funds. Being the cool Aunt I am, I committed to jumping in, but I had no idea what I was getting in to! He set himself up at a real desk with a notepad and a phone—he was the "Big Wig" and his sisters were his assistants, set up the same way, just across the room. I was blown away at the level of detail they put into acting out the reception area, right down to the judgmental expressions on their faces, their body movements, and the sentences they used. I was immediately transported into this make-believe world and didn't dare smirk or comment on it all; I was too busy absorbing what was going on and trying to keep up! So after the screening, I finally made it into the "Big Wig's" office. I froze when he looked me in the eye and asked me a very serious question, "Well . . . what do YOU want to do?" Whoa! When did he grow larger than life? This just got real! PANIC!

Here in make-believe land, I could do ANYTHING I wanted, and I was put on the spot, with 2 or 3 sets of impressionable eyes staring me down. These kids DO believe I can do absolutely anything, and they tell me so, all the time. The reality of the last few years of learning in my life set in. I know and preach how you have to be clear and focused and heart-centered on what you want, in all aspects of your life, but I still hadn't gotten solid on what I wanted to do, entirely, with my new life! I realized then, it was taking me a while to let go of any excuses I had for not going after every single dream I came up with. It sank in: This is NOT make-believe. I REALLY CAN DO ANYTHING I WANT! Gulp! My soul spoke up, as if coaching my voice how to say it out loud, "I want to travel the world and help people." There it was—I had admitted it, and I had an audience! As I sat there reeling at the whole experience, Mr Big Wig continued on, as serious as it gets, "Oh? That's interesting. And how will you do that?" Once you REALLY get to this reality, that you CAN do and be anything you want, it's overwhelming, to put it lightly, and I think that's why we panic and automatically want to run from it!

Still in a daze, I continued to let words just flow out, "Well, I like to write and share what I learn, so maybe I can go where people need help and write about it and get the word out, so other people that want to help know about it?" I was questioning myself and looking for his real acceptance, as I went. Man, was I nervous! God bless these kids for giving me some real practice! Later that day, he asked me if I was really going to travel far away. When I said I'd like to, he got all serious and said, "But not too far that you can't come back to us, right?" I reassured him I could always bring a plane home, anytime, and he seemed relieved. Ah, the reminder that I wasn't really "leaving anything behind." Ah, the love!

I admit I was still floating a bit above it all, as he continued questioning what my needs would be (a pilot- his little brother, who he interviewed later-- to get us there, the supplies, medical resources and other volunteers, financial donations, a website to follow my journey and social media to keep communications flowing both ways, the method to deliver on-going supplies, etc.). Then "his assistants" scheduled follow-up meetings with me where they gave me a booklet (a real, handmade booklet) providing maps, cultural tips, translation help, etc. On the cover of this booklet, after my full name, my niece had written, "I HoPe you Do grat at your New Job!!" How perfect is that? Inside, she threw in an "I love you," too. This is a keeper. Those rug rats don't skimp on the make-believing! WOW!

Again, the reality set it that there are ALWAYS people to help in whatever way needed—even kids 10 years old and under can figure out the details without blinking an eye! They were taking away any future excuses I could possibly come up with before I even had a chance! WOW!

Now when I was a kid, and truly, up until about a year ago, what I wanted to be when I grew up was much, much different, but I realize now that achieving any dreams gives me the experience and freedom to move on to even more dreams. In under 50 years, I had "mastered?" what I set out to do, from having a successful career and then my own business, to falling in love (more than a couple of times), to raising happy kids (and now a grandson! :), to establishing a home (again, more than a couple of times), to having several circles of good friends, and KNOWING there's more to life than we always thought.

But maybe most important of all, the traumas of my life have taught me what it is about me that makes me think these things were so important, and how the "outside" things do not matter at all. It's the INSIDE things—inside our very self, and connecting with the inside of others—that lasts. For instance, I'm inside a vast universe, not just inside a building I called "home." Everything and everyone inside any of the universes is connected, and every part of it is here for each one of us, no matter where we are within it, so wherever I am, I AM HOME. Home is wherever I am! It's a wonderful feeling, not feeling like I'm going to walk off the edge of the world and be lost, just because I don't have a "permanent" building I call my home that I feel I need to stay within.

SO KNOWING THIS NOW, I kind of have to let myself go and allow myself to discover more of my unlimited life potential, don't I? No matter what others think of me or what they want to do for their "normal life," my "normal life" is just about finding myself so I can be THAT . . . ever growing, ever changing, ever discovering, right? I tend to find myself easier when I feel I'm helping others, so I guess I need to continue doing that, too. After all, I always say, we are LIVING BEINGS, so we can never be doing nothing. Either we're living by allowing ourselves to grow, or we're dying by resisting and stunting our natural growth—it's as simple as that. So "What do I want to be when I grow up?" . . . TO BE CONTINUED . . . WOO HOO!!! :) *~Mary Anne*

LET GO OR BE DRAGGED!

Change  ***December 2015***

Some days, I don't know how I got here! The last several years are somewhat of a blur. I have some treasured memories in there, from happy to sad that I'll never part with, but what about the rest? It's been a whirlwind that I'm pretty sure launched me right off the planet more than once! Let me give you some advice up front: Remember, we can ask and pray for whatever we want, including, "to safely and gently slow things down." I didn't even think of asking for that until a friend recommended it recently. Thank God for the people in my life!

So how did I get here, in my brand new life, which still feels like a happy dream to me? It's been several months, and I still don't see anything or anyone stopping me from doing or being absolutely anything I want, except me! This is the truth of our reality, but it doesn't seem to be too easy to come by. We all have our share of struggles, often our whole life, but I hope I will always know to look beyond them from now on. I know the damage it can do if you don't, especially to your physical body, so if you feel tormented in any way, I can't tell you strongly enough to find another way before life has to step in and reset you! So now, I work on continuing to heal the effects on my body from my fast pace and allowing myself to be dragged too long, knowing the commitment alone is helping the various things that have dipped my health the last three years.

It sounds crazy, but the health issues are probably what finally forced me to move forward. For me, moving forward this fast could not have happened without **letting go**. If I had felt fine all the time, I would have had the energy to continue to enable people and situations that needed to change for the good of everyone. I also would probably continue to spend time doing things others wanted to do, but that didn't help me at all. I'm much pickier these days, knowing I have a limited amount of energy, thankfully. Not doing or being all you want is not only harmful to you, but to others as well, so these were some of the things I had to let go of:

- ✓ Doing so much for my grown, perfectly capable, smart kids and I helped them all move out and distanced myself a little to reinforce they are in control of their own lives and can do anything.
- ✓ The man I'd known for 10 years that I was sure I wanted to grow old with, when we became unhappy.
- ✓ Two dream homes in just a year's time, that I gave everything for. The first, built solely on my own blood, sweat, and tears and raised my kids in, and then the home I left that for, to someday retire with that man I had to later leave—two gorgeous properties anyone would die for. (This forced me to

learn I don't need to be in a specific building, or to be with anyone, to feel safe and at home.)

- ✓ Stuff I just didn't need anymore, as I did most of both moves mostly on my own, even the stuff I saved for, for years to have. It'll make moving around and traveling much easier in the future!
- ✓ Feeling like I needed to belong in certain groups. Belonging is fun and okay as long as it doesn't make you suppress who you really are, or hinder you from who you want to be and what you want to do. If it does, realize those people really don't care that much about you and will barely notice you're not there anymore. Trust me, there's a much higher percentage of people dying to love you for being your real self; they fall out of the sky when you start doing the things you know are the most fun for you!
- ✓ Trying to force myself into living a "normal life" as I realized that's a ridiculous thought, when each of us is born perfectly unique so that we can accomplish the special, non-standard things we are here to do! We are not born to be a clone of someone else! We are not born to live someone else's life!
- ✓ Thinking I "have" to do anything, like making my day job a top priority. Talk about selling your soul for money! Some experts call that prostituting! There's ALWAYS another way!
- ✓ Being the way other people want me to be, from how I dress and wear my hair, to what I do and how I act. People are still jealously catty, and often make up lies in an attempt to make you look bad, but I just

don't care anymore. Those people probably have a lot of growing to do before they can truly care about themselves and others. In the meantime, they show the world how much they lack self-love by picking on others, especially those just trying to help the world in some way.

- ✓ WORKING ON trying to let go of helping people that don't want to be helped, even if they say so; their actions tell us what their current motives really are. I need to respect their path, even if I feel they will likely struggle because of it. It's still their choice, so how dare I interfere with their learning!
- ✓ WORKING ON trying to let go of thinking things always need to be resolved, because sometimes they are not meant to be resolved, no matter how logical or simple it seems. Even when I see a rough road ahead, I'm learning to trust that people and things in life sometimes just need to take their own route, and that I need to be okay with possibly never understanding it! There's something for me to learn.

The magical thing about letting go is that once you commit to loving yourself and realizing your worth on this planet, your space is no longer filled with crap that needed to go, and THEN, there's room for the real things that are meant for you at this point in your life! Remember, as I let go of these things, I had no idea what I was supposed to do, or what my future would bring. I had to let go of the old habit of having a fear of the unknown—it's ridiculous too. Truly, I still don't have a clue, but the adventure is exciting, I have to admit! But once I cleaned my slate of the chaos and clutter, other things started blossoming and growing.

Without any effort on my part, I suddenly realized I had a strong desire to go south for part of the cold Wisconsin Winter. There was also little or no juggling involved, and no lack of funds or energy, every time I wanted to go to an event or take a class to learn something fun! I have incredibly real, respectful people befriending me all the time. My writing and project inspiration returned full bore; it's always effortless when I'm in a good place and I'm eternally grateful to have such an obvious gage. Everyone should do something creative that makes it so obvious when they're not taking good enough care of their life; it's much easier to catch yourself before you hit the murky bottom! Not happy? Change it or LET GO!!!

As I was finishing this article, I suddenly had a clear picture of my next book, a "Next Steps" guide, of which this will be the final chapter to celebrate my growth in the 5 years following the time I let go and opened my heart for all the world to see. I found the world to be a very kind place, when I just allow myself to be more of the real me.

Eternally grateful, *~Mary Anne*

TALK TO ME!

I would love to know what you think—about everything. I would love your feedback, your ideas, and especially, what other topics I could offer to help people? Please take the time to go to the publisher's website, ANNIEPRESS.COM, and follow the links to provide your valuable thoughts.

Also use ANNIEPRESS.COM to view more information on the author, the publisher, purchasing books, articles and video clips, additional projects, and how to contact us for anything you may need from us.

I plan to continue writing more books and articles, and to add short video clips to the website, so look there if you want more at some point. I also continue to work on several other projects (especially for children, teens, and wellness) and will provide links to those as well, on ANNIEPRESS.COM.

ANNIEPRESS.COM